MW01231233

It has been said tha
through the adventu
ers of Jesus. If you
update to Acts, this book is for you.

I have worked with Janet and Lana in the Philippines and Asia,
and I have seen their dedication to the service of the King. Their
submission and total obedience to the Lord is unparalleled. I believe
that when the eyes of God were running to and fro throughout the
earth in our time, he found the heart of these two precious ladies
perfect toward him. Every time they ministered, he showed himself
strong on their behalf. Doors in many nations opened wide, souls
were saved, lives were changed, communities were transformed,
leaders and churches were revived, and the kingdom of God was
advanced.

It is my prayer that this book will encourage you to be like Janet
and Lana—totally submissive and obedient to the Lord—so that
you will also have your own adventures with the Lord that will add
another chapter to the book of Acts.

—Rev. J. Boyonas
Church Multiplication Coalition Director for Asia

I have found both Lana and Janet to be powerful, gracious ministers
of the Lord. They encourage women to step out and be released in
their God-given gifting. This global connection has been through
Aglow International, a ministry that brought these two women close
to my heart as sisters in Christ.

—Edna Walter
Transformation Facilitator
Aglow International Australia

I met Lana Heightley and Janet Mangum in Kampala, Uganda. Since then, my ministry has never been the same. As a result of our divine connections, Janet and Lana have sent several short-term teams with the fruit of the Spirit to Kenya, transforming families in Africa. The outcome has continued to create divine connections for our global ministers. The apostolic anointing of these women, evident in the effects of the many teams sent to the nations, is greater than anyone I know personally. They are authentic and live what they teach. God bless you as you go through the pages of this book.

—**Rev. Stephen Osotsi**
Newsong Christian Centre
Nairobi, Kenya, East Africa

We got to know Lana and Janet Mangum at the first women's convention of Christ Faith Fellowship Philippines International. Since then, they have indeed made marks on the hearts of our women ministers and leaders. They have collaborated with us in many more conventions, not just with women and our leaders, but with the whole movement of CFFPI. Bishop Edgar and I are grateful and honored to have them partner with us in the building up of believers, most especially the women of the church, to know their place in the body of Christ. We treasure what they can do for his kingdom. Working with these ladies has been through divine connections.

—**Edna Reveche-Bantigue, Ed.D., JD**
Christ Faith Fellowship Philippines International

In 1999, two missionary adventurers, Janet Mangum and Lana Heightley, along with my wife, Cathy, persuaded me to join with Lana's brother Powell Lemons and his team on a two-week evangelistic mission in Bohol Province, Philippines. For us, it was like living in the book of Acts. I was hooked. Since then, I have continued to follow Janet and Lana's paths through the nations of the world.

We're privileged now to read the stories of their experiences working with God around the world. This book will encourage many others to co-labor for the Great Commission. Their example will stimulate faith and obedience for a new generation of volunteer missionaries. Who knows what God might do? Let's all continue with the heavenly vision along with them.

—**Jonathan Morris**
International Director
Church Multiplication Coalition

Having known both Lana and Janet for many years, plus having been a missionary in my earlier years, I can relate to so many of their adventures in Christ. Their lessons of growth, development, victories in spiritual battles, daring to do the seemingly impossible will inspire you even if you never leave your hometown. The evidence of God's grace will challenge you to cry out to God for the "greater things" that God can do in your life, if you will just say Yes. These two women have truly borne the fruit of apostolic gifts ,and their fruit remains as a living testimony. This is both a must-have and a must-share book for every believer. All things are possible.

—**Rev. Dr. Naomi Dowdy**
Founder Chancellor, TCA College Singapore
Former Senior Pastor, Trinity Christian Centre, Singapore
Speaker, Author, Mentor, Trainer, Consultant

I met Lana Heightley a little more than two decades ago at a women's conference in Mindanao, Philippines. I was stirred by the message she shared, and in my spirit, I desired to talk with her. Heaven orchestrated the possibility when she held my outstretched hand and brought me to the room where other ladies were seated. Her sensitivity to the Holy Spirit led them to pray for me and release a prophetic word, which eventually came to fulfillment.

Over time, Lana became close to my family's ministry as a mentor and spiritual mother. The grace of God in her life has continued to influence us to prevail in the work of advancing his kingdom, not only in my nation, but in many nations of the world. Our journey of love and relationship has brought eternal value, of which I am truly grateful.

I met Janet Mangum at the same conference. When she called for prayer, she asked me to stand alongside her to pray. I hadn't ever experienced such trust and confidence of ministering with somebody I didn't know. I believe it was a "Spirit to spirit" connection. I felt so honored to be connected with her, sharing the same passion for God and compassion for souls as our heartbeat.

When you discover the depth of God's love, then your relationship, purpose, and destiny can be achieved. You cannot afford to bypass the reading of this valuable book. These two amazing women are game changers.

—**Rev. Pastor Teresita Felicio**

GLORY
CONNECTIONS

Divine
Collaborations,
Challenges,
and Celebrations

REV. DR. LANA C. HEIGHTLEY
REV. DR. MELONIE JANET MANGUM

Foreword by Rev. Rebecca Greenwood

book**Villages**

ISBN: 978-1-94429-873-9

Cover and Interior Design by Scot McDonald
Cover image: iStock.com/ThomasVogel
Lana Heightley bio photo: Kristen Michalski

LCCN: 2020922129

Printed in the United States of America

1 2 3 4 5 6 7 8 9 10 2020 24 23 22 21 20

We dedicate these stories to all the global partners and team members we have served alongside through the years. Thank you, and may our Father in heaven return to you one-hundredfold of all you have given into the expansion and building up of the kingdom of God.

CONTENTS

FOREWORD

The year was 1992. My friend had purchased the book *Rees Howells, Intercessor* for me as a gift. I noticed that every morning when reading a chapter in the book, the previous night I had dreamt what was unfolding in the pages of the book. Only in many of the dreams, I discovered it was me having the experiences that I would read in the book concerning Rees Howells and his journey in the calling as an intercessor. It was evident the Lord was speaking, but I was uncertain of the fullness of what was transpiring.

One night I had a very vivid dream. Our oldest daughter, Kendall, was two. She was sitting on a pier, feet dangling off the edge, gazing down on the refreshing body of water below. I was watching her from the top of a hill and intuitively knew she was going to jump into that deep pond. I began shouting to two pregnant women who were supposed to be watching her, but my cries of alarm went unheard. I was deeply concerned because I knew she would not be able to keep herself afloat. I began to run down the hill toward the pier, shouting, "Kendall, baby, don't jump!" But the temptation of the cool water proved too strong, and eagerly she pushed herself off that pier.

Oftentimes the Lord will speak to us in a dream language that will be familiar. In my teenage years, I had worked as a lifeguard and swim instructor, so the scene in this dream would definitely strike a chord of understanding. I rushed to the edge of the pier and without hesitation dove in after Kendall. My baby was sinking under that deep, muddy water. But instead of being panicked, she locked eyes with mine. I noticed a distinct bright light, like the glory of the Lord, shining across her face. Even though she was sinking, Kendall was in total peace.

Because I had run so quickly, I was completely out of breath. One key that you learn in lifesaving is you can't save someone if you yourself are drowning. No longer able to hold my breath, I quickly swam to the surface, gulped in a deep breath of air, and pulled myself underwater to rescue my baby. It was the same scene as before. She was sinking with her hand outstretched toward mine, yet still at total peace. As the tips of my fingers touched hers, she suddenly slipped out of view, into the depths of the muddy water. This so startled me that I woke myself out of the dream, rushed into her room, and swept her up out of her bed into my arms and began to weep while rocking her back and forth.

This dream was beyond real to me. I felt I had lived it. For three days I ignored the Lord every time he nudged me to pick up the book and finish reading it. Finally, at the encouragement of my friend that this book and the life of Rees Howells had something to do with my calling of intercession to the nations, I decided to continue reading. I was nervous and questioned the Lord, "Lord, are you going to tell me I have to give up my daughter? Am I about to lose her?" As I read the next chapter, I was not encouraged. I discovered that Rees and his wife, Elizabeth, were called to Africa to birth revival. They had a precious baby boy, Samuel. He was eight months old. The area in Africa in which they would engage in mission work was too dangerous for a baby. Therefore, they gave Samuel to Rees' uncle and aunt to raise during the ten-year period of living abroad. Now I was really disturbed. I sat in my prayer closet and wept. "Lord, why did you give me this dream? Am I going to have to give up my child to go to the nations?"

The Lord spoke very clearly to me, "Becca, I am calling you to the nations. Where I have called you, I have called your family. You will have more children. But I am asking you to lay Greg, Kendall, and your future children on the altar and give them to me." My first thought was, "Here am I, Lord, send Greg!" My second thought was, "What will people think? I am a woman. Everyone will label me as a bad mother. Lord, can I wait until Kendall and my future children are eighteen?"

The Lord gently spoke, "Yes, you can. But obedience is better than sacrifice. If you will step in and begin to move toward your calling now, it will provide a righteous inheritance for your children and the generations to come. It will produce a hunger in them for the nations. Don't you know I love Kendall and your future children even more than you do? I can take better care of them than you while you are in the nations. My grace is sufficient. The choice is yours." Weeping as I lay prostrate on the floor of my prayer closet, I laid Greg, Kendall, and my future children at the feet of Jesus and said, "Here I am, Lord, use me." And twenty-eight years later, I have ministered in forty-five nations and seen the Lord move power-fully in the lives of people, cities, regions, and nations. And I can joyfully and gratefully give testimony to the fact that all three of our daughters love the Lord and each is pursuing her kingdom destiny.

You see, one of the most pointed truths that Jesus stated con-cerning our role in kingdom action is from John 14:12, "I tell you this timeless truth: The person who follows me in faith, believing in me, will do the same mighty miracles that I do—even greater miracles than these because I go to be with my Father!" (TPT). What a powerful promise and kingdom inheritance. It is exciting and awe-inspiring that Jesus calls us to do greater works than he did. As Jesus ascended to the throne room and the right hand of the Father, the Holy Spirit was sent to us. As believers we are empowered to do the work of the kingdom of God. Upon receiving our assign-ments from our King, we have the grace and anointing to implement them in our personal lives, in order to impact the lives of others and the sphere of influence we are called to.

Not only are we called to do greater works, but as his body, we are the fullness of him who fills all in all as Paul clearly states in Ephesians 1:19-23, "I pray that you will continually experience the immeasurable greatness of God's power made available to you through faith. Then your lives will be an advertisement of this immense power as it works through you! This is the mighty power that was released when God raised Christ from the dead and exalted him to the place of highest honor and supreme authority in the heavenly realm! And now he is exalted as first above every ruler, authority, government, and realm of power in existence! He is glori-ously enthroned over every name that is ever praised, not only in this age, but in the age that is coming! And he alone is the leader and source of everything needed in the church. God has put everything beneath the authority of Jesus Christ *and has given him the highest rank above all others.* And now we, his church, are his body on the earth and that which fills him who is being filled by it!" (TPT).

Within each of us is a longing to be part of something great. We all experience thoughts or even buried passions of wanting to be involved in a bigger plan—a plan in which the rule of darkness is shattered by goodness and truth. God placed that desire within us. We no longer have to feel as if our lives have little meaning. Our heavenly Father is about the business of reaping a harvest among peoples and nations. The beautiful scriptural promise is he has chosen those who believe in him to be his ambassadors and ministers of reconciliation. This is why I am so honored and excited to write the foreword for this awesome new manuscript, *Glory Connections.* Lana and Janet, along with their team members, have done a superb job in scribing their supernatural testimonies of great faith in which their simple childlike obedience has made a way for great spiritual effect of transformed lives of people, cities, and regions. Healing, supernatural protection, ministry relationships, and alignments forged that change and transform people groups and cultures. Cultural experiences that will draw you into the reality of the peoples and nations in which they have been called to. These women, whom I am honored to call friends, are history makers. These messages will draw you into the very presence of God, ignite a passion in you to experience and encounter him, and for many spark an awakening into kingdom destiny, where your cry will be, "Here am I, Lord. Use me!"

—Rebecca Greenwood
Co-founder
Christian Harvest International
Strategic Prayer Apostolic Network

THOUGHTS FROM THE AUTHORS

"It is vital for us to see and understand how God-given connections strengthen our lives." —Bill Johnson

"The first Christians were united by a bond of love. The Spirit brought about a holy connection—and this holy love held them together." —Lee Grady, *Set My Heart on Fire*

As team leaders who have partnered with one another's ministry, Women With A Mission (Lana) and Partners For Transformation (Janet), we have served together in churches and ministries around the world for thirty-plus years. Throughout that time, we have celebrated the glory of God generating upshifts in innumerable ways. We also found ourselves caught up in challenges within the teams themselves that could have defeated the work at hand.

Team Dynamics

A plethora of good books on leadership, conflict resolution, and teamwork is available that can enhance connections and collaborations in families or in ministry settings. This book, however, is not an exhaustive teaching on any of these topics. Instead, we share stories that illustrate the value of connections and collaboration adventures when you press through conflicts. In the end, we celebrate the Holy Spirit's interaction, for without him, we would never have these glorious stories to tell.

In Philippians 4, the apostle Paul asks others to help two women, Euodia and Syntyche, to resolve their conflict. Although readers have little insight into what was going on between them, Paul points out that reconciliation and unity of spirit are requirements for ongoing healthy teamwork and authentic personal witness.

Team ministry, by its nature, includes people who are diversely gifted. Every person has convictions about how ministry should evolve. These beliefs can, if allowed, create challenging conflicts and division. Differences in personalities, experiences, and worldviews in addition to differing spiritual gifts can bump up against one another. How these challenges are processed often determines how successful the outcomes are.

Keep in mind that even the best of friends can have conflicts with each other, the team, or a new culture or environment. Our challenges often relate with learning to respond in humility as we move together in the goodness of the Lord, extending every effort to live in unity while serving together in massive diversity.

Diverse Giftings

As we were gathering the stories for this book, Bill Johnson, senior pastor of Bethel Church in Redding, California, released his new book, *Born for Significance*. The opening chapter, "Welcome to the Conflicted Life," validates our norm in missions. He points out that conflicts aren't only external, difficult circumstances, but also internal struggles as we learn how this life in Christ is supposed to flow, especially in collaboration and connections in team ministry.

Both of us have learned how imperative it is to understand how people react to each other based on their personal motivational gifting, as described in Romans 12. The first book Lana wrote was a result of this discovery in team connections. *Presents from On High* provides real-life stories we both experienced firsthand to illustrate how each motivational gift interacts with the others in team collaborations.

Team ministry is the New Testament model for fulfilling the Great Commission. Jesus and his disciples worked together as a team during the three years of his ministry. As differences of opinion arose, they were dealt with and resolved. The apostle Paul tells us

THOUGHTS FROM THE AUTHORS | *19*

Jesus himself put together his team, a diverse bunch, for developing unity and maturity as they carried out the ongoing work of sharing the good news and making disciples out of the believers.

"So Christ himself gave the apostles, the prophets, the evangelists, the pastors and teachers, to equip his people for works of service, so that the body of Christ may be built up until we all reach unity in the faith and in the knowledge of the Son of God and become mature, attaining to the whole measure of the fullness of Christ" (Eph. 4:11-13).

Paul's ministry team was as diverse as the team of disciples Jesus had brought together. In fact, Paul's team encompassed members from two continents and crossed racial, social, cultural, and gender barriers. At a minimum, Paul's team included a theologian, an aristocrat, a prophet, a pastor, a businesswoman, a tentmaker, a doctor, and a teacher. His cultural intelligence needed to experience an upshift from the Holy Spirit to be able to fulfill God's commission in his life. His relationship with God was imperative to have effective team relationships that produced notable miracles (Acts 4:16) and enduring fruit (Luke 8:15).

Our teams have had the same level of diversity and likely similar challenges, as well as incredible Holy Spirit–enabled fruitfulness. Serving with the Holy Spirit's leadership is serving with the author of the Word of God himself. It's living and breathing his purpose in his ways as we live and move and have our being in him (Acts 17:28). We admit, we have missed a few steps here and there, but his grace filled the gaps.

Building a Successful Team

When we first began ministering together, it was our husbands, Tom and John, who talked to us about a key they had learned in business. They wisely helped us understand that when looking for team members, we should invite people who knew more about a particular area than we did, who had been given different spiritual gifts, and who had had responsibilities different than we had. Why? Because diversity is key to the success of projects.

Based on their encouragement, throughout the years we have intentionally invited men and women with a variety of speaking styles, knowledge, experience, and spiritual gifts to serve together. Little did we know the level of challenging conflict we were inviting. But as a result, we have seen the Holy Spirit's synergistic upshifts created from the personal and God-given uniqueness.

As time went on, the ability to recognize the value of unity in diversity led me (Lana) to form teams based on the members' personal relationship with me and my knowledge of their Holy Spirit–empowered gifting. Strong, effective, and life-transforming dynamics shared with each other opened doors for wildly effective ministry on every team, state, and country.

I (Janet) did not always have that choice. My team members came from a variety of denominations, churches, and even countries. Often, we met for the first time at the main international airport closest to where we were to minister. I had to access their God-empowered attributes literally on the fly. But being aware of Lana's teaching about how spiritual gifts reflect in personalities enabled a team-building synergistic wisdom. It helped us accept not only each other's extreme diversity in motivations and serving methods, but also enabled us to create an open forum for freedom of creative passion and purpose-filled and exciting interactions both within our team and with the cultures, ethnicities, and nations we came to serve.

Synergy

Our effective teams joined forces with one another's similarities and differences. We chose to lay aside our hunt for God's overarching will for our personal lives enough to make time to remember how much he cares about our responses to his Spirit's leading on behalf of those we are commissioned to reach. It can feel safer to commit to following him someday rather than to what he may be leading today. In fact, it is these very components that helped produce what has been our personal and Holy Spirit–empowered synergism.

Synergy is the interaction and cooperation of two or more that brings a multiplied effect. In our experience, team members achieved a greater effect than one could have alone. With synergy, the team was better equipped for greater impact. It was a challenge, but it was well worth it.

We want our lives to be filled with his Spirit to overflowing so that people would know the outcomes could only be empowered by the Spirit himself. He wants to take timid hearts and set them ablaze with strength and courage, so much so that people know something supernatural has taken place—life transformation just as miraculous as fire coming down from heaven.

As believers, we all have the advantage of both the risen Christ and the indwelling Holy Spirit. He is revealing his glory in unusual times and settings. Dependence on the Holy Spirit's leading glorifies our heavenly Father. It's not about working harder as much as it is getting ready for the Holy Spirit's adventures.

ALIGNMENTS FOR ASSIGNMENTS

Because He Said . . .

"For I know the thoughts that I think toward you, says the
LORD, thoughts of peace and not of evil, to give you a future
and a hope"(Jer. 29:11, NKJV).

"Since my youth, God, you have taught me, and to this day I
declare your marvelous deeds. Even when I an old and gray,
do not forsake me, My God, till I declare your power to the
next generation, and your mighty acts to all who are to
come" (Ps. 71:17-18).

*   *   *

I knew I had a future with God. When I was seven, my mother led
me in a repentant prayer. At age fourteen, I received my missions
call. From that time until now, I have had a sense of destiny.

Long before I went on my first mission trip, my mother was
my first mentor and trainer. I thank God for the powerful influence
God's women have on each other, which begins with mothers who
lead their children into discovering their destiny.

In 1986, I wanted to honor my father when he asked if I would
join him in Luzon, an island in the Philippines, for crusade meetings.
I agreed to work with him and my brother Powell, a pastor, for that
one mission trip. I thought I would be just a small part of a family
ministry. Little did I know that it would be a life-changing decision.

My First Trip

Along the journey of my following my call, several significant people became divine connections. I met two of them, Romeo and Nora Corpuz, on that first trip with my father. They were the first people I worked with outside of my own culture.

Nora was a pastor of a large congregation in the Philippines; Romeo was a bishop who also led an influential ministry called Life Evangelistic Crusade, which employed many pastors to work with partner missionaries. Romeo and Nora got their start in ministry as newlyweds, crisscrossing the countryside on a bicycle as itinerate evangelists. My father met them during a ministry trip and worked with them for nearly twenty years.

I will never forget arriving in Manila for the first time. The airport, small and outdated, was lit by dim bulbs hanging from the ceiling. The luggage carrier creaked as Nora and Romeo greeted us with wide smiles and big hugs. The first thing Nora said to me was, "Keep your purse in front of you and hold it with both hands." Nora's influence on me was just beginning.

When we got outside the airport, my first glimpse of the Philippines was of a sea of people, some on strange vehicles that looked like old U.S. Army jeeps. People crowded in on every inch of ground in front of me. As it happened, our arrival in the islands coincided with the military's coup over the dictator Ferdinand Marcos. It was a time of confusion, danger, and riots with angry demonstrations and celebrations all happening simultaneously. The international airport shut down the day after we arrived, so my trip lasted longer than planned. No international news was going out, and our families had no news from us for weeks.

Transportation from the airport to the mission base was an old-fashioned jeep, much like the ones I had noticed. It was called a jeepney. We were instructed to climb inside the open area behind the truck cab and were offered round cotton pads to be used as masks to cover our noses and mouths to keep out the dirt, grime, and insects. By the time we arrived at the base, our masks were black with soot, and we were oily from the dirt and humidity. Our eyes had mired circles around them. I soon learned that being constantly covered with soot would be the norm.

Even though our home base was only nineteen miles from the airport, it took us over two hours to arrive at Team Mission Compound. The congested traffic was nothing like I had ever witnessed. The streets had no defined lines for drivers to restrain their vehicles and very few traffic lights, regarded as merely a suggestion, not a law. The rule of the jungle was to keep moving and avoid looking at other drivers. The driver who went first got the open space, or the largest vehicle got the right of way. Above all, the drivers' communication tool was the horn, and they blared every mile of the way.

Apple Juice

Early the next morning, my learning began in earnest. Asking questions and observing became my occupation. Not wanting to embarrass myself or my family, I took notes on how people interacted with each other. What were the mannerisms and personal space requirements? Among other things, I learned that Filipinos could get twenty-five people in the same space of only five Americans.

For our first evening, Romeo guided our ministry team to a crusade meeting in a violently dangerous area. He would not let a small thing like revolution stop his call. He was a brave, bold man for God whose life had been transformed in every way. He and his family had been goons who carried M16 rifles and made their way by violence. When Jesus came into his life, Romeo exchanged his M16 for John 3:16.

At the meeting, I noticed he regularly would shout out, "Apple juice!" Sometime later, I asked him if he loved apple juice. He laughed and said, "I am not saying apple juice. I am speaking in my *Ilocano* dialect. I am saying, 'Apo Dios!' It means, 'Thank you, God!'"

That night was when I saw my first dramatic miracle, the first of many miraculous healings in the years to come. A woman's arm was crippled and frozen against the right side of her chest. As I prayed, I watched the Holy Spirit powerfully heal her. Her crippled arm began to tremble, moving away from her chest. Her arm was healed. I cried so hard and was so overwhelmed that Powell said, "Sis, you've got to get your emotions under control because there will be many profound miracles before we go home."

He was right.

A Dangerous Encounter

As we traveled back to our home base after praying for hundreds of people, Romeo and Powell were in one car. My father, his wife Wilma, our ministry partner and friend Betty, and I were in the other. Romeo was slowly driving farther away from us. I got a little nervous when I watched his little red car disappear.

It was usually safer to drive the back roads, but not on that night. Suddenly, we came up behind a logging truck that was stopped. It was so wide, it covered the entire road. What had happened to it and its driver? It was dark, late, and dangerous, so our curiosity wasn't lighthearted.

Suddenly, rebels from the political party that was defying President Marcos bolted from both sides of the truck with machetes in hand. They jumped up onto the logs on the truck and began fast and furiously hacking at the chains. Giant logs tumbled down the roadside.

Then the rebels noticed us parked behind them. One man picked up his machete and a long piece of the chain and came aggressively up to our vehicle. He pressed his face against the window in front of my father. We sat breathlessly still as he moved around to my rear window, putting both of his hands on the glass, trying to see what or who was inside. He suddenly pulled back, ran to the front of the car, jumped up and over the hood, and ran as if something had frightened him.

The minute he got over the hood, Wilma gunned the accelerator, pulling the car into a ditch, and skillfully drove around the logging truck. Within seconds, we were on our way back on the main road again.

After arriving back at the base camp, we excitedly told Romeo what had happened. He replied, "It is a good thing he could not see you. If they had realized you were Americans, it's a strong possibility they would have killed you rather than get caught stealing and logging."

It was well known that Americans were taking President Marcos out of the Philippines. So, the rebels had no love for us. We discovered logging was illegal on the island of Luzon, yet we were told Marcos allowed his cronies to log in the dark of night. Of course, they were sure he would get a few pesos for allowing it.

After further discussion, we all concluded that the man must not have been able to see inside the car. We believed God blinded him as in Genesis 19:11, when the angels blinded the men of Sodom.

On-the-Job Training

How does one try to explain the enormity of what I learned? I had so much to take in. On a practical level, I had to adapt to new foods. At first, I limited my eating to the peanut butter I brought from home and the wonderful local bread. I slowly adapted to their rice and chicken. Imagine my surprise to discover Coca-Cola and Spam had found their way to the islands. My favorite fruits were watermelon, pineapple, and the amazing mangos grown there. I also loved their *merienda* (tea times), but I never learned to adapt to *balut* and *durian*.

I also had to learn the meaning of cultural gestures and the need, when speaking, of eliminating idioms and colloquialisms. Every team of mine that has subsequently gone to that nation has had the challenge of trying to keep everything "close to the earth" and eliminating abstracts. Most of the time it is quite hilarious how the interpreter translates idioms. Other times, the use of colloquialisms can have serious consequences.

On one opening conference day, after I had been to the Philippines many times and had grown to love the people very much, I got up to speak. "I am so happy to be here. I truly needed my Filipino fix."

My interpreter asked me, "Fix? What is fix?" I pointed to my open forearm to show where a drug could be injected and said, "You know, like taking a drug."

She panicked and nervously said, "No, Sister Lana, please don't promote drugs with our women."

I also discovered the most important concept regarding time. In our culture, time is precise and structured. There, it is not. We think of following a schedule for events, but time is secondary for them. It is much more flexible. People are more important than time.

Over the years of our partnership, Romeo and Nora taught me many more aspects of ministering in other cultures. "Hot" cultures versus "cold" cultures, relationship versus task orientation, inclusion versus privacy, direct versus indirect communication, individualism versus group identity, different concepts of hospitality, and high context (formal culture) and low context (informal culture) all differ from place to place. All aspects are vital to understanding how people live out their values and customs.

A Fruitful Connection

After that first trip, I ministered with my brother and father in the Philippines until 1993, conducting crusades in primitive conditions: showering with no hot water (how I learned to scream!), sleeping on the floor on a one-inch camping bed with mosquito nets overhead, riding motorbikes, boiling water to drink, drenching myself in bug spray, and ministering in *nipa* hut villages. It was hard, hot, and humbling.

In 1993, I mentioned to Romeo that I noticed a program of systematic training for women did not exist. I told him of my desire to do that training. He shouted, "Yes! We have been praying for that for many years. Hallelujah! Let's do it."

Subsequently, I took my first team of twelve women to the Philippines in 1994. God worked miracles, and both the women on the team and the Filipino women began to believe they could do something meaningful for God.

I am so thankful Nora and Romeo were patient and long suffering with me to enlighten my mission-world knowledge. My connection with them has been more like a family relationship than a friendship or partnership. Each of our lives has changed. Because we merged with each other in like-mindedness and purpose, the face of the Philippines has been greatly enlarged for the kingdom.

Together, under the power of the Holy Spirit, we have achieved supernatural successes. Hundreds of thousands of souls have come into the knowledge of salvation. Miracles have been the norm. Hundreds of churches have been planted. Thousands of men and women have been trained and empowered.

My path and destiny have been immeasurably influenced by Nora and Romeo. The years of our ministry partnership have truly been a fruitfulness of working together to expand the kingdom of God

"Apple juice! Apo Dios!"

*   *   *

The following is Ptra. Lenora A. Corpuz's (Universal Pentecostal Church Inc. Meycauayan, Bulacan, Philippines) story:

Philippines Connection

The Women with a Mission (WWAM) Ministry in the Philippines was a tremendous blessing to us women—women who found the answer they were waiting for, women who had stories to tell, tearfully displaying the joy, freedom, enthusiasm burning in their heart and soul.

No doubt the WWAM Missionaries were ever on fire preaching, teaching, lecturing with courage, with devotion and love overflowing, they were filled and anointed by the Holy Spirit. Their gift and calling, their passion for the cause of women seemed to have no end. The Filipinos loved them, admired, and longed to see and hear them, indeed, they were gifts from heaven.

When the Life Evangelistic Crusade was launched by the late Bishop Romeo Corpuz Sr., one of the very first missionaries who came was Lana's family. This is where it all began with passionate crusades, conventions, conferences and meetings with God's miracles and wonders.

Lana's and Janet's very meaningful and touching teaching on the "Wedding of the Lamb—Here Comes the Bride" will not be forgotten. The Spirit of the Lord moved mightily and we were immersed in the power of God. Dynamic encounters occurred as they passed through the prayer tent rededicating their lives to their Bridegroom Jesus in a beautiful veiled wedding chamber. The whole place seemed to be shaking with His presence. It was an illustration of the hope and promise of redemption.

When we were in the northern part of the country in Pangasinan or Tarlac, the local church prepared a nice bamboo hall close to the church. After the first part of the meeting, we needed to transfer, but the presence of the Lord was so strong the people would not leave. The worship, praises, dancing were non-stop for hours. What a sight to witness. All of the women were on fire with joy unspeakable and gladness in their hearts. They were bare footed and perspiring, but felt so much love and care for God and for one another it was incredible.

Another event I want to share is our conference meeting in Benguet, Baguio City the summer capital of the Philippines. Normally during summer, water is a serious problem in the City.

During this time, there was no rain for months so that draught was felt in the whole city. People were hungry due to the dry rice fields. This created a serious problem when managing the convention. A surprise and wondrous thing happened when the team arrived at the venue—rain started pouring down. Janet and another team member, Lynn, took off their shoes and began dancing, rejoicing and praising God in the downpour. It made everything fresh. We were hopeful and thankful because God knew the great need. The people kept uttering, "They brought the rain! They brought the rain!" Needless to say, we had a great number of delegates, far more than expected. There was little potable water and the heat was really challenging after the rain. The team and delegates were devotedly firm and ready glorifying and honoring Him in the midst of all the challenges.

It was a continual work of the Spirit of God in signs and wonders. It was evident that joy and contentment filled their hearts to be more on fire for Him. It did not matter how hard and uncertain things were at the time for the simple reason that Lana and Janet and their teams loved Him and loving Him meant loving us, too. We, therefore, salute you, team leaders, Dr. Lana Heightley, Dr. M. Janet Mangum, and every woman that came on those teams. We love you and are praying for you. Maraming, maraming salamat po, pagpalain kayo ng Diyos! Many many thanks and God bless you richly!

You, Too

"But in fact God has placed the parts in the body, every one of them, just as he wanted them to be. If they were all one part, where would the body be? As it is, there are many parts, but one body. The eye cannot say to the hand, 'I don't need you!' And the head cannot say to the feet, 'I don't need you!' On the contrary, those parts of the body that seem to be weaker are indispensable,

*and the parts that we think are less honorable we treat with
special honor" (1 Cor. 12:18-20).*

* * *

**Have you witnessed God starting a work that has grown and
flourished over the years? What role did you play?**

....

Melonie Janet's Musings

Yes, I can do it; you can do it.

Now, let's enter in.

God wanted it; Jesus gave it,

So we could begin again . . .

To know his love and make it known . . .

To walk in the power of his Spirit . . .

Flesh of his flesh and bone of his bone.

....

Lana's Leadership Lines

God brings the increase. He is the multiplier.

My times with these godly people prove that what we do is
not all about what we achieve in the brief but powerful times
together. It is as much or more about what we have set into
motion. God's ways are cumulative over the years, each blessing
building upon the other. This truth is why we have the same
passion for planting seeds as we do for reaping the ripened fruit
when it is picking season.

* * *

*Thank you, Father God, for aligning my heart with new connec-
tions for your glory. May the fruit of my past giving bring forth
abundant blessings in the kingdom of God.*

Mentoring Collaborations

Because He Said . . .

"A voice of one calling in the wilderness, 'Prepare the way for the Lord, make straight paths for him'" (Mark 1:3).

"Jesus looked at them and said, 'With man this is impossible, but with God all things are possible'"
(Matt. 19:26).

* * *

My first two evangelism-focused trips into the Philippines working with Pastors Powell Lemons, Romeo Corpuz, and Jill Boyonas were pivotal for my future. They were generous gifts of encouragement, wisdom, training, and support.

One afternoon, Pastor Jill took me and fellow teammate Jerry into the *barangay* to share Jesus with people. Jerry wanted to do all the talking and praying with people, which did not give me any space. So Pastor Jill decided to split us up and have another team member go with Jerry. The pastor ended up coming with me.

We ended up under a tent in the open-air market. It was hard to get anyone's attention on a one-on-one basis because of the busy, noisy atmosphere. Then Pastor Jill asked me to preach. Not only were people saved that day, but a lady who could not move her fingers asked for prayer, and before our eyes her fingers started to move, and she was healed. When the crowd saw the miracle, many asked to be prayed for, and we had an instant healing line at the market.

It was later that night, after Pastor Powell's evening evangelistic message, that Jill spoke to me. "Janet, you can do this."

I wondered what he meant. Surely, he wasn't talking about leading a team and being the main speaker.

He continued, "You have the anointing to be the lead evangelist, and I can see God would empower you to lead a team. Find some team members and consider returning as the main speaker."

I could hardly believe what I had just heard. Me? *Oh, Father God, is that true?* Inside I desperately hoped Pastor Jill was seeing what I did not yet realize. It was an invitation into the Holy Spirit's leading in my life.

Know Your Audience

I was still in a massive learning curve when I took the team from Malibu, California, as the main team leader. I had the faith and the biblical knowledge, but I learned that was not all I needed.

It was to be my first time speaking before thousands of people; it was also my first time preaching an evangelistic message in the Philippine culture. I stood staring into the gathering of thousands of men and women patiently waiting for the opening announcement. My heart pounded with desire to impact their lives and to please God. Hearing my name reverberating through the immense speakers, I had a giant grin on my face as I jubilantly bounced to the microphone.

What was my message that evening? I don't have a clue. I do remember being a bit surprised when the interpreter flowed along with me, with barely any hesitation. Since I was the guest speaker, Romeo, the local evangelist, gave the invitation to receive Jesus. When he bellowed the passionate invitation in his native language, my chest vibrated with the power of the Holy Spirit. I had never experienced anything like it. The impact was unmistakable. Then in English and Tagalog, I heard him roar in a deep, anointed voice, "Run to Jesus!"

Chairs tumbled over as the crowd rushed toward us. I stood stunned, watching people race toward the stage, their hands raised, their eyes filled with determination and desperation. Healing miracles poured over the thousands at such a rapid pace that we couldn't keep up. What words can describe such a surreal experience?

I didn't sleep much that night, thinking about the glorious miracles I had just witnessed. I was desperate to learn how to have that level of impact.

"Please, Romeo," I asked, "how can I improve?"

He was caring and honest as he responded, "Don't ever do that again."

My heart sank, but I mustered up courage to listen to and receive his admonishment. "It's a good thing I was your interpreter," he continued. "I knew what you were trying to say and interpreted your heart in concrete terms. I used words they could relate to through their senses, rather than abstract concepts that speak only to the intellectual understanding of a concept."

Seeing my sincere desire to learn, this gracious evangelist continued giving me examples of when I had been too abstract, assuming the audience would understand what I meant. He pointed out my use of the words *fire* and *passion*. "Don't just bounce the ball with these metaphors of friendship, honor, or even religion or love. Shoot for a basket with concrete truths by telling stories illustrating each concept."

In that watershed ministry conversation, I realized that the night before I had given a message without thinking carefully about the lifestyle of the listeners. I swallowed the embarrassment as best as I could. Trying not to look too devastated, I humbly thanked him for his advice.

The next day it was my turn to speak again. Was I scared? Yes. Worried? It goes with scared, right? I not only wanted to please

God, but I also desperately wanted to please this incredibly anointed evangelist. I believed his advice was constructive and prayed that my words that night would make a difference.

Thankfully, my message that evening did its intended work. That trip was a landmark discovery. It has continued to impact the way I share the love of our heavenly Father and our personal Lord and Savior. I have had the privilege of being mentored by each of these pastors. Pastor Boyonas has been an ongoing, life-altering connection. The Holy Spirit has continued to connect me with good mentors. Listening to their heartfelt wisdom in character, messages, and teamwork has transformed my leadership. I am forever thankful the Holy Spirit led me into these life-changing connections.

You, Too

"To the weak I became weak to win the weak. I have become all things to all people so that by all possible means I might save some"
(1 Cor. 9:22).

* * *

Has the Holy Spirit led you to wise mentors? Is it time for new connections?

Melonie Janet's Musings

Listen, learn, lean. Liberally follow his lead. He is developing you and your team. Outside your paradigm, but within his design, connections will align. It's a key to communication that will multiply transformation. It changes how you feel and what you say. Lean in, listen, and obey.

....

Lana's Leadership Lines

Know your listening audience as much as possible for effective communication. Do the needed research as well as tap into the wisdom of the local leadership.

* * *

Thank you, heavenly Father, for the pivotal relationships in my past. Thank you for the ones you are connecting me with in the future.

New Covenant Partnership

Because He Said . . .

*"I have called you friends, for everything that I learned from
my Father I have made known to you" (John 15:15).*

*"Holy Father, protect them by the power of your name, the
name you gave me, so that they may be one as we are one"
(John 17:11).*

*   *   *

Friends and followers of Jesus experience more than the Holy Spirit's
gifting and power for daily living and ministry. They also are given
connections with other believers to help them fulfill their destiny
to build the kingdom of God here on the earth. My team ministry
in Africa came about through what seemed like a random meeting.

A Fortuitous Connection

Pastor Adonia spoke on a Sunday morning at the church in
Southern California where my husband, John, and I attended. He
was from Uganda where he had a formidable ministry, going to
unreached villages to take the good news. He loved going to those
who had never heard the name of Jesus. He had come to the United
States to share what was happening in Africa and to invite the
church to partner with him in executing this harvest work.

John was taken aback by Pastor Adonia's message. Being a

relatively new believer, John did not fully understand the concept of reaching unreached people. The very idea that there were people who had never heard the name of Jesus was disturbing. After Adonia's presentation, John leaned over to me and whispered, "I want to take that man to lunch." So we invited our pastor and Adonia to join us.

What a lunch it was. John was so moved with Pastor Adonia's story and compassion that he wanted to partner with Adonia's ministry—not just in giving, but in going. John asked if we could possibly go there for a one-year tour. "Of course!" Adonia replied. Although it was a year before we went there, John was invited to be on Adonia's ministry board.

Years later, as Adonia was returning to Uganda after another visit to the States, his plane was shot down by terrorists while flying over Rome, Italy, leaving us for heaven. Shortly thereafter, John was asked by Pastor Adonia's board to go to Uganda to assess the health and condition of the ministry. He agreed. While there, John worked with a young man who was one of the pastor's close disciples. John determined this young man to be of spiritual strength and a servant leader who carried the same vision and anointing as his mentor. His name is Godfrey Saazi Mesweige.

John learned that Godfrey had no formal education but spoke ten different African dialects. During a long-distance phone call with me, John suggested that Godfrey establish his own ministry. John also said that he would support Godfrey to go to a Bible college for training. I agreed, and both things happened. The ongoing covenantal partnership had begun.

John and I continued to invest in Godfrey's life. He was, and is, my Ugandan son. We have achieved so much together, and we have shared other ministry connections and networks with each other. Through strategic partnerships, we have benefited greatly in our work for the kingdom. Many of these partnerships are interwoven in our relationship.

Eleven years after my initial introduction to Godfrey, I took my first training team, including Janet, to work with Godfrey in Uganda. It was a team of fearless women, each one with a serious heart for discipling the nations. Our training included working with both men and women leaders. Godfrey gathered them from the Democratic Republic of the Congo, Rwanda, Sudan, Somalia, Kenya, Ethiopia, and Uganda for the conference training.

A Clash of Mighty Voices

Proverbs 9 speaks metaphorically of wisdom mingling its spicy wine. Godfrey and his team, alongside me and my team, mingled together with the national leaders in attendance. I thought of Matthew 9:17, new wine being poured into new wineskins. Together, we were a highly seasoned mixture of experience and anointing, gathered in a new wineskin container of God's making, ready to be poured out so that everyone present could experience the glorious presence of our Lord Jesus.

During these meetings, we saw miracles, healings, signs, and wonders. Even with so much success, early in the sessions our team experienced a nagging feeling that something was off. We noticed attendees occasionally slept, seemed distracted, and were restless. The meeting room at times felt spiritually suffocating. It lacked the vibrant joy of being in the presence of the Lord and worshiping him wholeheartedly. We were in the presence of Christian leaders whose once passionate, dedicated voices had taken a turn to a sober silence. They had lost their jubilant sound.

How could these dedicated, sacrificial servants of God be so weakened? Could it be that unfulfilled desires had dulled their enthusiasm? Was it the heat? Were they tired? Did they not understand our teachings? Could it be that deep disappointments had spiraled into hopelessness, stifling their spirits?

After one event, I asked Pastor Godfrey to give me a deeper overview of the attendees. Were they all faithful leaders or pastors?

How would he assess their relationship with the Lord? What did he think was going on?

It became obvious to Godfrey and my team that those attending wondered if they would ever feel spiritual fulfillment and the freedom to valiantly love and be loved like they once had. We felt a mixture of compassion and grief for them.

When I stood behind the pulpit to speak, I was so grieved by the atmosphere that tears began to flow down my face.

Oh, dear God, we must have breakthrough! I prayed.

The whole team of speakers sitting nearby immediately joined me in prayer, crying out to our Lord Jesus, raising our voices in tearful laments: "Help, restore, deliver!" "We don't know the circumstances that have plummeted these leaders into this dreary, oppressive slump, but we know they need you, Holy Spirit, to comfort, restore, and deliver." "Empower our voices to help them receive a breakthrough of hope and faith, and once again have powerful encounters in your loving presence."

Suddenly, with great emotion, a woman lifted her hands to heaven and shouted, "Lord, forgive us!" The whole room then erupted as the Holy Spirit moved through the room. People cried out in repentance and asked for renewal, seeking God with a sense of urgency. Loud screeches, smashing of chairs, and kicking ensued as evil spirits fought to keep the people's voices silent in the depressed crowd. At one point, approximately forty people had come down to the front near the pulpit and were struggling with a demonic presence. Nevertheless, in the chaos of it all, the host of evil spirits was defeated.

What an incredible experience for our team to watch the sovereign and powerful Father God, Lord Jesus, and Holy Spirit exhibit mercy and restoration as God's love prevailed. As our team prayed, praised, and spoke, the power of the voices of faith, combined, transformed lives.

What we experienced that day was a clash of mighty voices—the enemy's voice trying to hang on, disrupt, and disorient, and God's voice triumphing through his servants and the Word of God. In a miraculous, dynamic, and powerful moment, the atmosphere changed. Worship burst from the people's hearts, coming from all corners of the room. Freedom rang in their voices as unbound leaders expressed their gratefulness for God's personal and merciful presence.

One in Spirit

During the team's remaining time in Kampala, we went into the surrounding villages with Godfrey. We ministered to the staff in the governmental offices in the city, where one man recovered sight in his right eye.

Africa's worldview is mainly one of fear and power. People in villages are especially fearful of evil powers. A notable miracle was a confrontation between Godfrey and a witch doctor, also the village chief. Several tribal men began to levitate. With complete confidence in the name of Jesus, Godfrey shouted out to them, "Come down in Jesus' name!" All of them fell onto the ground and were apparently unable to get up. It came as quite a shock to some of the audience, but it was not unusual to Pastor Godfrey. What a powerful demonstration of the name of Jesus against the forces of evil.

That day, all those watching realized that Jesus was the greater God. Since our God was stronger than theirs, they were ready to listen. We freely shared the good news of the kingdom of God and the love of Jesus for them.

The partnership between Godfrey and my teams has continued to expand into partnerships with other ministries. In addition, Godfrey now ministers around the world as a bishop for his church. Salvations, church plantings, notable miracles in healings, deliverances, and trainings of African pastors and leaders as well as those in other nations continue to this day.

One of our ministry friends and partners, Pastor Jonathan Morris of Church Multiplication Coalition, reported watching as Bishop Godfrey prayed for a man's emaciated leg during a ministry event in Haiti. The young man had been born with one normal leg and another partially formed leg with the foot not attached normally. In less than a second, bones, muscles, and connective tissue formed, and the man was able to stand on two legs. He didn't feel anything happen, forcing Godfrey to repeatedly ask him to look down. After he walked, he started to run, and ran to his mother's house. The next day, more than two hundred people received Christ as a result of the miracle.

Godfrey and I now meet up in countries around the world to work together, and he calls me Mom wherever we go. Our partnership has displayed family and oneness. We have mingled the truths God has taught us. We share friends, family, and spiritual principles. We are one in Spirit and life. Our connection is a beautiful one. A powerful one. A life connection.

Your voice as a believer in the Lord Jesus is powerful. Whether it is expressed in a whisper or a shout in the spirit realm, it makes a difference. When you express the love of Father God in any measure or manner, the very sound of your voice is impregnated with the sound of heaven. You are his instrument, his building, his temple, his trumpet, his megaphone, his clarion call—his voice in the earth.

You, Too

"For the eyes of the LORD range throughout the earth to strengthen those whose hearts are fully committed to him" (2 Chron. 16:9).

* * *

Is it time for you to make a full first commitment to your Lord and Savior, unlike any you have made before? What about a renewed commitment?

·····································

Melonie Janet's Musings

FEAR THE LORD

Tremble, tremble, quiver, shake.
God is moving, twirl in his wake.
Reverence has taken hold of flesh.
The soul is strong in quietness.
To the marrow, rejoicing has filled the bones.
The reality of God's goodness is being made known.
I stand at attention in his holy presence
with every sinew vibrating with the Father's resonance.
His Word runs swiftly through the land.
By his Spirit I have followed his command.
The God on the mountain lives in me
that his Word may be revered,
not as in the days of old when
Mount Sinai shook, and the people feared.
Now it is I that shake in God's presence,
no longer afraid but filled with reverence.
Jesus, my heart is jubilant in your excellency.
Thank you for your love and sweet liberty.

·····································

Lana's Leadership Lines

God gives power to his obedient sons and daughters. We are to subdue and rule over all the enemy's work. God is looking for people who are not self-centered, who do not desire to build their own kingdom, followers who are not under the disillusionment of power but of love to serve the peoples of the earth. He wants servants who are worshipers and warriors who want righteousness to flourish. Partnership sometimes involves clashing worldviews on everything from food to matters of faith and practice. As we humble ourselves, prefer others above ourselves, honor them, and issue grace, God brings amazing results. He desires humble servants who do not care who gets the credit.

May we sing, "With your blood you purchased for God persons from every tribe, and language and people and nation" (Rev. 5:9).

* * *

Lord, I thank you that I have authority in you to participate in the building of your kingdom. It is being established through all peoples. I acknowledge the reality of your goodness. It is being made known in all the earth.

BREAKING LOOSE

Because He Said . . .

"Therefore, if the Son sets you free, you really will be free"
(John 8:36, HCSB).

"The man from whom the demons had departed kept
begging Him [Jesus] to be with Him. But He sent him away
and said, 'Go back to your home, and tell all that God has
done for you.' And off he went, proclaiming throughout the
town all that Jesus had done for him" (Luke 8:38-39, HCSB).

*   *   *

Have you ever ridden on a speed-blasting, flipping, and twisting roller coaster that spins you in a delirious 360 degrees? You look down and your knuckles are death-grip white. Everyone around you is wide-eyed, screaming at the top of their lungs. As a teenager, I couldn't wait to get on those roller coasters, but my body didn't agree. Swirling up, down, and around until I abruptly landed on the ground once again, I would wobble off, run to a nearby trash can, throw up, and get on again.

I've decided this willingness to get right back on must have been part of my preparation for ministry. There have been trips when the challenges were so overwhelming, it felt as if my head was spinning. I would dare to lift my hands in the air, praising God as we zipped around the next curve. Slowing to a stop and getting ready to go home again, I would mutter, "I'm never doing that again." Before long, however, the grace would reappear, the longing to serve would set in, and I was off on another ride in the Spirit with my Lord.

Dramatic manifestations, intimidating demons, and drastic transformations all occurred on one of my African roller-coaster rides. Sounds crazy, doesn't it? And it was. No fake or exaggerated news here. This is my story, and it's true.

Around the Next Curve

I was intrigued when I opened the invitation to speak at a women's conference in Zambia, Africa. I was ready for a new adventure in another collaboration and Holy Spirit–initiated connection.

Out of my sense of capability seems to be the refrain of my life. Here I was in Zambia, there again. It's not my preference to travel to a nation by myself, but I had no choice. My confidence was a bit shaky in my ability to cross over the cultural barriers. But, as always (as if I had a choice), I trusted the Holy Spirit to make the difference as I gave a valiant effort following his leading.

After leading a team years before, I had called Lana, and with a whiny, pleading voice, had asked her, "How do you do it?"

"Do what?"

"Find things to talk about with leaders when you have little or nothing in common."

She laughed. "Janet, you can do this. Just talk about the Lord, his Word, or the working of his Spirit."

I knew she was right, and on this trip, I did my best, but the awkward feeling inside didn't dissipate. I was the only stranger among the speakers. I kept asking the Holy Spirit, *How do I navigate these days filled with awkward conversations during break and dinner times?*

What do you do when you feel blank and out of place? Do you refuse invitations or hide away in your room whenever you can? I don't like admitting it, but I have hidden myself in a room in years past. You know as well as I do that none of these choices stems from the right motives. They show a lack of understanding of God's nature or your own personhood in Christ. It was time again to trust the Holy Spirit for whatever was around the next sharp curve.

Stepping Out in Faith

The last speaker finished, and the conference was concluding for the night. I had thankfully fulfilled my role and was relaxing in the front row, feeling quite comfortable now with the local pastors. The ministry leader then asked me to join her in praying for the women on stage. They were lining up by the hundreds for her to say a blessing, which was going to take hours without help.

Why not? I thought as I stood. I began praying a simple blessing over these women who were hungry for the equipping of Jesus' grace in their lives.

I reached for the first one, but before I barely got close enough to touch her, or say more than a couple words, down she went onto the floor. And she didn't even seem conscious. I watched for a few seconds, and she seemed comfortable lying there. I looked around at the local pastors. No one reacted with more than a smile, so I reached for the next woman. Flop, down she went, half lying on the legs of the first woman.

Now what, Lord?

Again, they seemed peaceful, so I kept praying. One after another took a dramatic and startling plop on the floor until we had no room for others to pass by. Some of the women were criss-crossed on top of the others with hands and legs in disarray.

Father God, you must have done this. It's up to you to finish it.

I turned to the main leader and asked, "Don't you have leaders who can pray for these women and move them out of the way so we can pray for the others? It's getting too crowded up here."

Four pastors in the front row jumped onto the stage and began praying and lifting the women to consciousness, escorting them to another room to continue ministering in whatever the Holy Spirit had begun.

"Next," I invited. As the woman stepped closer to me, she hurled backward as if hit by a blast of hurricane-force wind, and I hadn't even touched her. She collapsed in a heap of contorting demonic manifestations. Not a pretty sight.

I scanned the row of leaders. "Who has experience with deliverance?"

One confident-looking lady calmly nodded with bright eyes and a wide smile. I asked, "Could you take her to a private place to set her free?"

The woman tagged two other intercessors to lift and carry the contorting, demon-afflicted woman out of the auditorium. I turned to focus on the hundreds patiently waiting for their turn.

It's mind blowing to step up, step out, and watch God transform an atmosphere. I was privileged to minister and, at the same time, be a spectator. In the moment, it feels so natural, so normal, but later you can't help but marvel.

The hours flew by, and the room grew quieter, more meditative, with soothing worship music playing. The women began to amble back to their rooms with arms around a friend, holding hands, or leaning their heads on a shoulder.

Freedom in Jesus

I sat meditating on this precious gift from heaven that had happened, when one of the pastors asked, "Would you like to experience a deliverance our way?"

"Absolutely."

It was 11 p.m. and time for another sharp turn on the roller-coaster ride. She led me out the side door to a giant succulent-looking *baobab* tree. One lonely light had been strung from the building to a low-hanging branch. A harried-looking young woman sat slumped under the tree with a blank stare into the dark night. Her dirt-smeared face looked as if she wasn't aware we were there. Her dress was ragged with a few rips and tears. As we approached, the deliverance pastor began to take authority in Jesus' name over the demonic realm that had held this woman captive. This pastor knew the young woman personally, as well as the witch doctor she served. The pastor understood the demonic names that had not only harassed but tormented and enslaved this girl in satanic ties with this witch doctor.

Deliverance from demonic torment wasn't new to me. I had prayed for eight hundred to one thousand people by that time and had seen the beauty of freedom overtake their souls as Jesus set them free. In my travels, I have been part of the ministry leadership in various cultures, setting people free in the powerful name of Jesus. That night, once again, I had the honor of being an eyewitness to the undeniable authority of the name of Jesus Christ defeating the darkness every time the demonic realm was challenged. As each demon left, the girl let out a long scream. She wildly rolled like a ball bumping downhill over the rocks under the tree, her clothes tearing, while the next evil spirit was making its last attempt to torment her. But Jesus' name always prevented the demons from remaining or harming her.

The complete freedom wasn't immediate, but considering the level of demonization, it wasn't long either before she began to feel the peace and presence of God overwhelming her soul. She was exhausted, her hair matted and sticking up in every direction, dress ruined, but quieted and stunned. We helped her to her feet. The pastor walked her to her room, softly singing to her.

She had come to the conference to be set free. She had heard about Jesus and wanted to receive him as her Lord and Savior. Jesus knew her heart and her captivity. Without us knowing why she had come, she was able to sit in the conference, which was a miracle all by itself. She came forward for prayer that night. There wasn't a sign at the time that would lead us to believe she had been so demonized, but Jesus knew. Jesus was there for her. He set her free.

Beauty from Ashes

We had one last gathering the next morning. The atmosphere had completely changed. Their newfound liberty, in both soul and body healing, was evident throughout the audience. Tears of relief flowed. Smiling and laughing emerged from every section.

The gatherings had gone from feeling oppressive when we first began to feeling like the morning calm after a typhoon's downpour and lightning storm. This particular morning was a time for testimonies. One after another, the attendees continued to share their encounters with the Holy Spirit healing, delivering, empowering, and inspiring. The testimonies declared healing from physical and emotional pains. It was astounding to hear the tangible manifestations of the Spirit of God displaying his splendor. I felt deeply thankful, celebrating his mercy and grace.

A lovely young woman stepped up on stage. Her face was actually shining. I knew she had experienced something incredibly wonderful, and I couldn't wait to hear her story. She began by describing how she had been bound with numerous demons tormenting her. But the night before, Jesus had set her free. You could see her testimony in her face as she bounced and twirled in sheer delight.

I turned to the pastor next to me and asked, "Is there more to her story than she shared?"

"You don't recognize her, do you?"

"No, should I?"

"She was the one we prayed for together last night to be set free."

I was shocked. This girl's supernatural makeover was so striking, I didn't recognize her. That's what you call a complete transformation of spirit, soul, and body. It was an honor, a deep privilege, a supernatural manifestation of God's glory. Only he could have accomplished such beauty from ashes, such joy from mourning. He had reclothed her in the Spirit of his hope and resurrection power rather than heaviness, captivity, and pain.

You, Too

"How could one man chase a thousand, and two put ten thousand to flight . . . unless the LORD" (Deut. 32:30).

"A man who endures trials is blessed, because when he passes the test he will receive the crown of life that God has promised to those who love Him" (James 1:12, HCSB).

* * *

Have you ever noticed when you minister with other believers of like mind, heart, and purpose, there is an increase in authority? Do you have an inner circle of faith-filled friends?

....

Melonie Janet's Musings

Often when perseverance finds a way,
It looks back upon its path
And discovers—lo and behold—
It was not chance when it took its stance,
But the way was appointed from of old.

....

Lana's Leadership Lines

Spiritual authority is increased as we team together. A powerful synergy is created when two or three agree. Look for those who are of like faith, and join together when standing against the forces of the enemy.

* * *

Lord, bring those into my life who have a heart to set people free. Teach us how to work together in unity. Anoint us to expand the kingdom of God. I declare Jesus is Lord.

LEARNING TO FLY

Because He Said . . .

"But those who wait on the LORD shall renew their strength;
they shall mount up with wings like eagles, they shall run
and not be weary, they shall walk and not faint"
(Isa. 40:31, nkjv).

* * *

When the Holy Spirit comes upon a group of believers, they must be open to expect the unexpected. This truth can be far more evident in cultures outside the United States because of their openness to the unseen world.

Team member JoAnne has mentored me for twenty-four years in ministry as a friend, advisor, and board member. A former regional director of Aglow International, she is a groundbreaker and pioneer who has served her state and local church as an advisor, teacher, and inspirational leader. Her longevity in business as well as ministry in the Christian community has enabled her to empower God's people to move from the church into the marketplace with influence and excellence.

She also travels globally to train pastors. People of all ages are inspired and released into their destiny as JoAnne ministers in the gifts of wisdom, prophecy, and words of knowledge. Her gift of teaching and storytelling warms hearts as she shares her experiences with passionate transparency.

Here are her thoughts on the Holy Spirit's gifts and ways, along with a story of an experience in the Philippines.

∗   ∗   ∗

The following is JoAnne's story:

JoAnne's Story

Most faith-filled believers readily embrace the motivational gifts described in Romans 12. These seven gifts, as functions of the indwelling of the Spirit, are automatic and received at salvation. Christians like having these basic gifts as a primary driving force in their lives. They feel natural, explainable, and orderly, reinforcing their identity.

The motivational gifts encourage believers to be servants. They go on mission trips to build buildings and meet other practical needs. But the motivational gifts are just one aspect of the Holy Spirit's gifts. The other part—the supernatural, anointed, empowering part—manifests when the Holy Spirit comes upon believers and anoints them for ministry.

The supernatural workings of the Holy Spirit are an essential part of all Women With A Mission ministry teams. Those on WWAM teams quickly realize they must be flexible, aware, and open to spontaneity. Anything can change in fifteen seconds. The why, the when, and the how of the Holy Spirit are unpredictable. To operate in these gifts requires a deep trust in God and a deep trust in one's teammates.

I saw the work of all these gifts as a member of Lana's team. On a recent trip with Lana to the island of Boracay in the Philippines, we heard a young man call out, "Momma JoAnne! You taught me to fly!"

I turned toward the voice and saw Daniel waving. Immediately, my mind went back to fifteen years earlier on the island of Cebu.

A Special Night in Cebu

Daniel was sixteen years old and part of a traveling worship team. More than seven hundred men, women, and children had gathered in an open-air building to attend the weekend conference where Daniel's team was serving. The large concrete building was to be their sleeping quarters at night and classrooms by day. Outside the building, big vats of soup and rice were perched on open fires. Clumps of bananas hung in a tree, waiting to be eaten. The area had been experiencing a major drought, and the people were hungry. Our team hoped they would be as hungry spiritually as they were physically.

It was extremely hot and muggy. Pungent smells of body sweat and damp hair filled the air, and our team's loose-fitting cotton dresses clung to our sticky bodies like spandex. When a team member stood up after sitting on a metal chair, I would reach out and tug on her hem to pull her dress loose from her buttocks. We were a comical sight, but we didn't care. We were on a mission.

Filipino worship music has a unique sound—and it is loud. Daniel's thunderous pounding on the bass drum caused the singers' voices to become even louder. The Holy Spirit must have loved it, because his presence filled the room with a thick haze hovering about two feet above the crowd.

Sarah, one of my team members, said, "The Holy Spirit just told me we are to run around the room and throw water on the people."

We never questioned how it might look—we just did it. We all grabbed bottles and ran, splashing water onto the crowd, declaring an end to the drought. The people clapped, laughed, and rejoiced with us.

I then walked onto the platform and whispered in Daniel's ear, "God wants to help you make these drums talk. To soar. To prophesy." His eyes grew wide in wonder. "Listen to your heart,

Daniel, and find his rhythm."

I placed my hand on his shoulder and waited. Softly, he began to tap on the drum, searching for the sound of the Lord. The crowd leaned in to listen as the air became even thicker with the presence of God. The drumbeat built to a crescendo, as if calling out to the crowd to come up higher in their faith. Everyone stood up, rising in unison as if an orchestra conductor had signaled them with his baton. They clapped to the rhythm and lifted up praise to God.

Suddenly, Daniel stopped playing. The people stopped clapping. A holy hush followed. A powerful sense of God's glory was felt throughout the room. Some people trembled under the weight of his presence, some fell to the floor, some were filled with deep joy, others had visions, and still others received emotional and physical healing. The Holy Spirit ministered to each individual at the same time, in a place of their need—an experience no man could ever provide. Minutes later, his presence lifted. The people began to yell out what they had experienced.

"The tumor on my chest is gone."

"The big lump on my neck just shriveled away."

"I've struggled with depression for years, and I felt it leave me."

"I just got saved!"

"Look, I no longer need my crutches. I just got healed!"

These exclamations represented only a few of the countless lives changed that night by a divine encounter with the God of the Bible. What happened was a beautiful demonstration of the Holy Spirit coming upon a whole room of people. They experienced what Scripture speaks of in Acts 2 when the followers of Jesus were gathered in one accord, in one place, and God's presence filled the whole house.

That night was forever seared in Daniel's memory. Fifteen years later, standing on the shores of Boracay, I heard him say, "Momma JoAnne, I've never forgotten the miracles and your teachings on becoming an eagle Christian. I still have flashbacks of that amazing night." With a wide grin, he laughed. "You taught me to fly!"

Unbeknownst to me, Daniel had pulled a thread from my mantle, my anointing, and with the help of the Holy Spirit, it was woven into his. Now an associate pastor, he is teaching many on the island how to live in the realm of the Spirit. They are learning to mount up as eagles—to be flexible and move with the leading of the Holy Spirit. With the eyes of an eagle they, too, are soaring to new heights—learning to discern and observe both trouble and opportunities afar off.

Now, whenever I pray for Daniel, I often envision young eaglets fluttering and beating their wings. Their efforts might be a little rough at first, they may even fly into a tree or two, but wonder of wonders, they, too, are learning to fly.

You, Too

"He shall cover thee with his feathers, and under his wings shalt thou trust" (Ps. 91:4, KJV).

"Now Joshua son of Nun was filled with the spirit of wisdom because Moses had laid his hands on him" (Deut. 34:9).

"Do not neglect your gift, which was given you through prophecy when the body of elders laid their hands on you" (1 Tim. 4:14).

* * *

Are you ready to fly? What could that look like?

Melonie Janet's Musings
ALL CREATION SPEAKS
I want to be God's butterfly, a wholly new creature
propagating my faith in Jesus as his rabbit
with the strength of his bull,
the fight of his cougar,

the endurance of his roadrunner,
the flight of his eagle,
the beauty of his rose and the freshness of his dew,
with the song of his lark,
the wisdom, thought, and eyes
set not on any of his creation,
but only on HIM!

Lana's Leadership Lines

The Spirit of God is the essence of his presence inside of us that urges us to dare, to release ourselves from the earth's demands and soar free to the dwelling place of God. Impartation is a biblical principle. It has to do with giving and receiving of spiritual gifts for the work of the ministry. It is the transference of each gift from one man or woman to another.

* * *

Father, I worship you with my whole being—body, soul, and spirit. Help me to burst free from those things that hold me down and help me to ride the wind of your spirit. I desire to soar on your wings.

God's Purpose Prevails

Because He Said . . .

"A person may have many ideas concerning God's plan for his life, but only the designs of his purpose will succeed in the end" (Prov. 19:21, TPT).

"But the plans of the LORD stand firm forever, the purposes of his heart through all generations" (Ps. 33:11).

"I know that you can do all things, and that no purpose of yours can be thwarted" (Job 42:2, NASB).

* * *

I met Melanie Boudreau at a women's prayer retreat and immediately knew she was a woman of passion and determination. I didn't know about her intense love for God and prayer, but I was drawn to get to know her more. Eventually, she traveled with me on a team to India.

Mel is now a partner and team member. She is an incredible intercessor who has become a trusted friend. Her wisdom far exceeds her years. She travels with and sometimes leads teams for me in addition to the ministry she pursues to the nations on her own.

This time traveling with Janet's team, here is how God used her on a trip to Myanmar in an unexpected way for his purposes.

The following is Melanie's story:

Melanie's Story

Empowering women has long been Lana's heart's cry, as well as Janet's. At the core of Women With A Mission is raising up and empowering women to go to the nations. Lana could not possibly lead teams to all of the places where Women With A Mission is invited to teach and disciple, so part of Lana's role is to help train leaders, build teams, develop financial support for them, and oversee them as they go.

In November 2014, I traveled with an evangelism team of women to Myanmar. At the time, I was in my fifties but one of the youngest women on the team. We had been invited to partner with pastors of small churches in Myanmar. Local believers in Christ often experience harassment and persecution, so our team expected to experience the same.

In this nation, which is semi-closed to the gospel, hassle at inspection stations was common. To protect our original travel documents, we carried copies of our passports to show at the myriad of the checkpoints. Doing so ensured that no overzealous officer who confiscated a copy of our credentials could trap us in the country. Amazingly, because our traveling vans were full of older women, we appeared harmless to the authorities and quickly passed through with few questions asked.

Even though I had spent many years desiring someday to minister outside of the home, that experience in Myanmar made me realize that those gates were now opening to me without opposition. The older I got, the greater the opportunities afforded to me would allow me to minister in the nations that were the hardest to access, the very places my heart gravitated.

Our American faces drew crowds, and our association with the local hosts granted them both credibility and clout. Our esteem and respect for them encouraged them in their ministry as well. We were pleased to serve in whatever way they desired. Open evangelism is not allowed, so we engaged instead in cultural exchange, meeting in the homes of villagers. In this predominantly Buddhist country, an entire "church" rarely consisted of more than fifteen believers in Christ.

Going out in groups of two along with an indigenous translator, we spent our days in stilt homes, describing the context of our lives. "My name is Melanie. I live in Colorado. We have very high mountains and lots of snow. The most important thing in my life is my relationship with Creator God, the Most High." My brief introduction would serve as the beginning of a gospel presentation that ended with prayers for salvation and then prayers for healing for any medical issues in those present.

Each team member went to a host home filled with local neighbors. On one occasion, about twenty neighbors crowded into my host's home to hear the gospel. Several attendees responded to the message, desiring to give their lives to Christ. After the gathering, our host indicated that she would escort us back to the rendezvous point with the rest of the team, which was several blocks away. On the way she diverted, insisting we visit her dear friend who was unable to walk because of a terrible injury—bones shattered in her ankle.

My partner and I attempted to lay hands on the woman's foot, but she shrieked in pain. Instead, we held our hands a few inches away and prayed for God to heal her. Within sixty seconds, a smile enveloped her face. God had miraculously healed her ankle. She stood up, amazed, testing weight on her leg and beaming with great joy. Our host then translated for us as we shared the gospel and led the grateful women to faith in our powerful God.

The next day, the plan was the same, but in a new location. This home was larger, and the local Christian congregation attended in full force, about fifteen strong, along with another dozen or so unreached neighbors. Two of the Christian women needed healing—one was blind, and another was partially paralyzed.

"I am going to see the blind healed," I predicted excitedly, full of faith.

As I shared the good news of Jesus, many responded, but inside I was distracted the entire time by the next activity on the agenda: prayers for healing. When that time arrived, I prayed, but nothing happened. Crestfallen, I wrestled internally with God. In response, I felt the gentle nudge of the Spirit invite me to do a mini-teaching on bringing God glory in the midst of disability, not just through divine healing. Either way, God was glorified. A life lived with a disability has value and dignity as much as one without it. I knew this truth because I had raised two children with disabilities and had recently published a book about it.

As I spoke, I could feel God's brilliance. These women with disabilities were being validated in an honor/shame culture and in front of their pastor, congregation, and prominent members of their community. The smiles on their faces at the affirming conclusion of my lesson matched the face of the woman the day before who had experienced physical healing. At once, I realized that who I am had been forged in the crucible of my home life, raising my children, while crying out to God for his sufficiency.

Our God forges his message in and through all those who surrender their lives to him. His purpose prevails.

You, Too

"After this the Lord appointed seventy-two others and sent them two by two ahead of him to every town and place where he was about to go. He told them, 'The harvest is plentiful, but the workers are few. Ask the Lord of the harvest, therefore, to send out workers into his harvest field'"
(Luke 10:1-2).

"All of your troubles can be utilized to comfort others with the same comfort you have received from the Holy Spirit"
(2 Cor. 1:4).

* * *

How have you seen this truth in your personal life? How has it made a difference?

....

Melonie Janet's Musings
PETER
Sift him like wheat, the devil cried.
Keep his faith sorely tried.
Before he can begin to feed the sheep,
Let's drive him into utter defeat.
Aha, but remember,
when the devil's boast rings in your ear,
Jesus himself prayed for you so you need not fear.
When faith's full working turns you around,
strengthen your sister and brother so they can abound.
No longer can he (the devil) sift—no longer profane.
You're seated in high places by Jesus' blood and Name!

....

Lana's Leadership Lines
God uses our everyday living to train us for ministry. Steadfastness is the quality of being resolute, firmly fixed in place,

immovable. God forges steadfastness through difficult times. Our disappointments and challenges can be building blocks in forming stronger teams able to work together, appreciative of others' time, making them feel important. They can enable teams to have authentic relationships as they serve together in the expansion of the kingdom of God.

* * *

Heavenly Father, thank you for loving me. Thank you for the mercy of my Lord Jesus that enables me to live and move and have my life flowing in the Holy Spirit. Thank you for turning my life around, filling me with purpose and sending me to those in need of the same comfort and wisdom I have needed throughout my life.

ROCKS, SNAKES, MOSQUITOS, AND BRIBES

Because He Said . . .

"Dear friends, don't be surprised at the fiery trials you are going through, as if something strange were happening to you" (1 Pet. 4:12, NLT).

"Who shall separate us from the love of Christ? Shall trouble or hardship or persecution or famine or nakedness or danger or sword?" (Rom. 8:35).

*   *   *

My husband, Tom, is a pilot. He understands what action needs to be taken if the plane begins to stall and descend in a dangerous, less-controllable condition. To recover from a stall, an experienced pilot will reduce the angle of attack. The plane recovers its lift and continues its route.

My team's journey in Uganda had at least four major stalls. They weren't uncontrollable, but they did demand immediate attention, fast thinking, and faith in God's provision to keep us moving forward.

Gaining Altitude, Experiencing Turbulence

By this time in ministry, my emotional awkwardness with the local culture had taken a back seat. I thought the adventures in various countries had prepared me to be ready for whatever surprises we would face. Today, my definition of being prepared has been wisely transformed. Being prepared no longer means I am trained to handle any situation. It doesn't mean I know I have all the survival tools I need either. Now, being prepared means I have done as much as I know to do. The most important preparation is that I am fully dependent upon my heavenly Father, Jesus my Lord and Savior, and the guidance of the empowering Holy Spirit.

Who can describe the feeling you have when you are greeted at the airport by the local team who has been patiently waiting for your arrival? It's electric with wide grins, big hugs, and hearts filled with anticipation. We had connected with local pastors and leaders serving together to bring life and an upshift in the Spirit for their people.

The welcoming information began as my co-leader Fran Hallgren and I, with our exhausted team, piled into the transports. The upscale hotel was air conditioned and had delicious buffets waiting for us. So far, our journey was everything we had hoped it would be with all the luggage arriving and our ministry connections found with ease. Little did Fran and I know how many stalls were going to try to impede our journey.

We enjoyed a full night's sleep, hot steamed milk in a big cup of African coffee served in fine porcelain, and fresh pineapple, guava, and papaya that filled the breakfast table. Fran and I sat there like children waiting to be escorted into their favorite theme park. Our hosts arrived to take the whole team to the conference. The men were dressed in their regional *kanzu* clothing. The women were adorned in brightly colored, crisp, elegant *gomesis*, with matching buttons and accessories. What a drastic difference from the torn jeans and crumpled linen tops worn by the young leaders where I live.

The anticipation in the air was so thick, it felt as if we could reach out and touch it. The days' schedules were filled with dancing, praising, teaching, and preaching. The presence of God made it clear it was his will to bring life. Hundreds came forward to receive the infilling of the Holy Spirit and began to praise God in supernatural languages sent from heaven in each event setting. His glory and goodness filled the days with indescribable, notable miracles.

Tired but exhilarated from the honor of serving the people for days with God's purposeful presence, it was time to head out for our next event. A few hours' journey into the heat of day, our first stall tried to crash our upcoming events. The van's tire blew wide open as we bounced over a large rut in the road. We had traveled quite a distance inland with no place to repair a tire for miles around. The area was primitive, and the scorching heat suffocating.

Before we had a chance to recover from our first stall, the next critical stall demanded we reduce the angle of attack even more, find a place to rest, and wait. Stacey, one of the team members, had been bitten by numerous mosquitos the night before and was so weak she could hardly hold her head up. We spotted a shaded wooden cover with rugged, backless benches to wait out our time.

We spread an old blanket on the dirt so she could rest quietly. The heat of the day turned into cool of the night and still no sign of a new tire. These stalls tried to usurp our joy as well as interrupt our ministry opportunities.

The search for a reason to smile took intense focus. It would have been normal to feel faint, fearful, and frustrated while we sat sweating, lamenting our losses into nightfall. We made a gallant effort to look peaceful and full of faith in expectation of God's upcoming provisions. After all, our hosts were doing the best they could to provide for us. We didn't want them to feel guilty or worried more than they already were.

Finally, hours later, a new tire arrived. I sat in the back seat with Stacey's head on my lap, trying to ease her misery. We bumped down the road with such vehemence, her head would bounce inches off my lap, while the driver swerved to miss as many ruts as he could manage. Praise God, we arrived and got her into bed. Thank God, she slept solidly all night.

Another Dip in Elevation

The next day Stacey was up and ready to minister in the out-reaches. Our local ministry hosts, however, insisted that it was important to check to see if she had malaria. Stacey, the two hosts, and I rode to the local clinic that evening. The rural clinic was much simpler than our urgent care clinics in the States.

We had a myriad of unspoken questions. *Is the needle sterilized? How about the cotton balls? They don't look clean.* Feeling a bit nervous about what was around the next corner, Stacey bravely gave permission for the nurse to draw blood for a test.

We sat on the hard metal chairs in the outside waiting room for the results. The doctor called us into his office. As we listened to his diagnosis, another stall startled us. I looked down at the floor between the doctor's desk and where we were sitting and thought I saw a small black snake. No one else seemed to notice, so I figured I would quietly mention it.

"I think that's a snake, isn't it?"

One minute our hosts were sitting quietly, but in the next two seconds, with panic-stricken faces, they both jumped as fast as accomplished gymnasts up on their chairs. Our angle of attack was about to drastically change.

The doctor threw his chair backward, his long legs leapt from behind his desk to the top. Jumping down, he bolted out the door. Stacey and I just sat, staring. He swiftly came back with a broom and violently began sweeping the snake out the door in a frantic and fierce attack. We could hear loud shouting in another language and banging with something metal on the tile floor. Apparently, they killed the snake with whatever was available. It seemed so small, but they obviously knew it was dangerous.

The doctor calmly returned. We had lift again and were safely returning to our original missionary journey.

"That was a venomous black mamba snake, and even when young, if it bites you, you could die in a moment," he casually mentioned.

A Long Delay

Rural adventures can have extreme highs and fast-dipping lows. We altered our angle by praising God for being our experienced pilot, saving us from stall after stall that could have crashed our ministry times. In every stall, God provided a restorative lift. After his restoration of time and health, we stepped into another expression of his love for his people. Each day had a potential crash, but each day we saw him lift and restore.

Have you ever been through drastic challenges in a short period of time that could have devastated your future, but instead you experienced God turning around the negative situation in the end? Like us, you realized you passed through the shadow of death into the provision of the light of life himself. Now, looking back, you celebrate the lifts and upshifts that kept you going. Me, too.

Safe and headed for the airport to return home, we were again celebrating God's goodness when a police checkpoint stopped us. Rested and ready, with our luggage packed, we had no clue we would experience another stall in our journey. Our driver didn't have a driver's license. The worried faces of the police revealed the lack of documentation.

As we were pulled over and waiting, the 92-degree African sun heated our van like an oven. We began to wonder if it was possible we could miss our international flight home. We had little to drink, no food, and no store nearby. Sweating, thirsty, hungry, and longing to get on our plane, we began fervently petitioning God for help once again. We discussed what angle of attack was best for this stall. Was this a spiritual attack? If so, we decreed, in Jesus' name, God was making the way where there was no way. Was it no more than a circumstance common to a journey? Either way, we chose to rest in our heavenly Pilot's expert hands.

We asked God, claimed his promises, sang songs of praise, and encouraged one another until we were exhausted from the effort to remain hopeful. How could we transform this stall into a joyous ride? The time had come when praying in our Holy Spirit–given languages, described as tongues in the Bible, was the best angle of attack.

Fanning our red, perspiring faces, we could hear the incessant chattering between the driver and the local police. We couldn't understand one word, so we intently scanned their body language. Were they expecting money to let us go? Would there be an enormous fine? Our driver apparently thought it might work. I have been in countries where a monetary gift was expected, or paying the fine now, but not in this case. He offered a bribe, and then we were in real trouble. Angry words were flying from the police, aimed at our driver.

As if the rest of the issues weren't enough, a team member got a bad cut on his foot and could hardly walk. Since we had been in the hot sun for hours, one of the women began to feel weak and faint. We were exhausted and cranky. The team was valiantly trying to keep from showing their distress. We purposed to remain in faith that God was helping us handle the challenges, and he would get us where we needed to be in time. Again, we continued to lift up prayer in our supernatural languages to quiet our souls.

At times, these things happen. Compared to other stories I have heard, these inconveniences were minor. What do you do? You stop, adjust your lift, keep going, keep believing, keep trusting, keep petitioning and declaring the Word of God over the circumstances. Whenever you can, you sing his praises and search until you uncover a way to laugh.

How did it get resolved? We were never told. As we piled back into the vehicle heading for the airport, we sighed in grateful relief. It wasn't easy. It wasn't fun. But you can imagine how thankful we were when what seemed impossible turned around for good.

After flying for two days in and out of airports, we were snuggled in our own beds back home once again. Did it all happen, or was I dreaming? It seemed so surreal compared to home. Hundreds blessed by God's goodness, healed, and delivered; others challenged, and yet recovered. Rocks, flat tires, a snake, mosquitos, and a not-so-wise bribe didn't stop God's life-giving presence displaying his splendor.

I pray I am never in a plane that stalls, but these ministry stalls were well worth the fast falls and gave me a story to tell, how God worked through it all.

You, Too

"Therefore do not worry about tomorrow, for tomorrow will worry about itself. Each day has enough trouble of its own" (Matt. 6:34).

"All of them were filled with the Holy Spirit and began to speak in other tongues as the Spirit enabled them" (Acts 2:4).

"You need to persevere so that when you have done the will of God, you will receive what he has promised" (Heb. 10:36).

* * *

Have you asked the Holy Spirit to fill you with the fullness of his presence, including any and all of his gifts?

Melonie Janet's Musings

Spiritual words form Spirit-born prayers targeting his will. When heaven kisses earth through the tongues of angels, interventions from the Holy Spirit are invaluable.

As I was praying in the Spirit, the Holy Spirit whispered these words into my soul:

Hold tight. Keep the Light. Stand firm and learn. Breathe deep. Christ will keep. Position yourself upon the Word. Pray in light. Await to be heard. Undrape and unfold; miracles to behold. No more strain; only God's refrain. Awake to surroundings. Behold adventure. Possess your new land always in tenure. No glancing, no prancing, only repose. Lift up; look up. God is ever present and near. His transforming power is changing your life this very hour. Do not fear.

Lana's Leadership Lines

Leaders trust God through challenging circumstances. They don't cave in. They believe the Holy Spirit is leading the way. Is there anything too difficult for God? What can impede the plan of God? Leaders choose to believe what they know is true in difficult circumstances (Job 42:2). They know the plan of God cannot be thwarted, so they endure until the end.

* * *

Father God, you are a good father. I believe that means you are the God of restoration and transformation. Thank you for turning what the enemy meant for evil into something that not only glorifies your good fatherhood, but redeems our lives from destruction.

SIGNS AND WONDERS

Because He Said . . .

*"Then Moses stretched out his hand over the seas; and the
LORD swept the sea back by a strong east wind all that night
and turned the seabed into dry land, and the waters were
divided" (Exod. 14:21, AMP).*

*"He let loose the east wind from the heavens and by his
power made the south wind blow"
(Ps. 78:26).*

* * *

Our lives in Christ have unexpectedly been punctuated with signs
and wonders. Clouds have swiftly turned another direction. Winds
have ceased or changed course. Connections and invitations that
we could never have arranged on our own keep weaving in and out
of our ministry adventures.

Protection and provision for the will of God to be accomplished,
in any given moment, can be startling. We continually find ourselves
staring in awe and praising God for who he is and his willingness
to intervene in supernatural ways. We've seen enough to convince
us that when we don't see the answer, we can remain in faith,
trusting the One who loves us more than we can imagine.

The Strong North Wind

There we were on the island of Siquior, Philippines, standing on a stage in a concrete building dotted with openings for a cool tropical cross-breeze on a hot, humid island day. The eight hundred session attendees were seated, waiting for the program to begin, when a thick substance began to pour through the south side windows. The building began to fill with heavy smoke.

We could see people beginning to itch, cough, and sneeze. Experiencing uncomfortable chest issues, the worship team struggled to sing. What was going on?

A spiritual battle had been activated since our ministry team had landed. Our research had revealed that this particular island was known for its spiritual darkness and had experienced defiling bloodshed. We had planned communion for the end of our sessions, trusting the blood of Jesus to counteract the defilement.

The local witchcraft practitioners were trying, once again, to curse the event by interrupting our worship and ministry time by sending smoke-filled curses our way. How did we know? You would have to have been there to experience the knowledge that came from the Spirit of God. We asked the local leaders to make sure we were hearing right, and they confirmed our suspicions. Sure enough, it was a common witchcraft practice to burn a collection of items while commanding the smoke to disrupt and irritate any Christian gathering.

Simultaneously, we voiced the same thought. "Let's rebuke the curse and declare God's power over the wind!" We looked at one another and simultaneously shouted, "Moses!"

Together, we held up our hands, remembering how Moses held up his staff against the water until it miraculously parted, so God's people could cross over the Red Sea in safety. We commanded together, "Wind, come from the north and blow the smoke out the windows, away from this crowd."

Suddenly, a north wind began to blow through the upper

windows. What followed wasn't a slow dissipation of the smoke, but a dramatic expression of an act of God. Immediately, the wind changed, blowing the smoke out the same windows from which it had entered in a matter of a few seconds. The smoke took a dramatic sharp turn, 180 degrees, back toward the ones who were sending the curse. What a glorious sight! God had made his point and power clear.

The rest of the team on the stage seemed unaware of how the Holy Spirit had just been their advocate. Worship, teaching, and preaching continued with no more interruptions.

We believe in the power of Jesus' sacrifice on the cross, often referred to as the blood of the Lamb, which releases the supernatural authority of Jesus in the spiritual realm. As the session continued, we believed our prayers for cleansing the land would be a sign against the forces of darkness in the name of Jesus.

Communion

Our plan for the communion time in recognition of our personal relationship with Jesus included prayer for the cleansing of the land. Our local hosts, Tessie and her team, had prepared the communion elements. When the time came to serve them, we reminded the audience of the value of the covenant of the blood of Jesus and the life he sacrificed on the cross. Scriptures began to flood our thinking, validating the act of praying in faith for land cleansing, as in Leviticus 18:1-25, Jeremiah 19:2-5, and Ezekiel 16:24-27.

As we declared that heaven would invade earth, we broke the elements in half, taking communion together. We instructed the audience to spread out around the property outside the meeting hall and pray against the evil that had been perpetrated there in the past (Zech. 3:9). It was a sacred time as they prayerfully poured out the other half of the grape juice and broken bread over the land.

I (Lana) prayed aloud, "Dear Lord Jesus, forgive the past sins of the people of this land, and bring cleansing, sanctification, and redemption into the physical property as well as transformation in the lives of the residents."

That act was a significant operation of the Spirit of God on behalf of the land. We have received reports of enduring impact on the island since that time.

A year later on another island in the Philippines, a similar witch-craft attempt was made to interrupt an evangelistic outreach event Janet was leading in the Philippines. More than four hundred people had gathered in another concrete building with no air-conditioning. With sweat pouring down our faces, we stood on a hot and humid evening surrounded by a suffocating, massive insect population.

The videographer, David, was attempting to get quality footage. From the stage, the team could see him swatting at annoying swarms of bugs that landed on his face and clothes. At no other location had there been that dense a concentration of insects, and it was unnerving. Despite all odds, David valiantly managed to capture good video.

The next day was Sunday. Team members went to churches all over the island to share God's love and purpose. As Janet reclined, enjoying a refreshing bite to eat with the local pastors after the service, she asked, "Is it possible the overwhelming bug population last night could have been a work of witchcraft rather than some-thing natural?"

One of the pastors answered matter-of-factly, "Yes, of course. They put bugs in a jar and curse them to go, interrupt, and irritate Christian gatherings."

If you've never heard of such a thing or been present when witchcraft tried to defeat the work of the Holy Spirit, this statement may sound wild or ridiculous. Ask those who live in settings that experience these spiritual battles on a regular basis, and you will find it to be somewhat common.

Janet asked the pastor to drive the team by the same building they were in the night before. As they approached the building, they decided to rebuke any curses that witchcraft would use to distract or irritate in any way. They even "blessed" the bug population, commissioning the flying and crawling creatures to cooperate with God's heart for his people.

Hundreds gathered again in the hot, humid building that night. David was the appointed speaker that evening. We wanted to get good footage of him speaking because he was so generous to us the night before. Janet put her hair in a ponytail, in case there would still be a few annoying insects as she got ready to do the filming. As long as she didn't shake the camera too much, she could swing her long hair from side to side, using it like a horse's tail to swat at the flying bugs.

While David spoke, we kept scanning the room to see what God would do. We were expecting the bug population to be less miserable. However, as the evening progressed, we were stunned repeatedly—the myriad of insects had not merely decreased, the air was completely empty. It was a sign and wonder.

That night God had made sure we knew it was his hand of love and power at work. These workings of the Spirit of God are called signs and wonders because they are *signs* of his loving presence and caring that cause us to *wonder* in awe of his mercy and grace.

You, Too

"The wind blows wherever it pleases. You hear its sound, but you cannot tell where it comes from or where it is going. So it is with everyone born of the Spirit" (John 3:8).

"God also testified to it by signs, wonders and various miracles, and by gifts of the Holy Spirit distributed according to his will" (Heb. 2:4).

"Again, truly I tell you that if two of you on earth agree about anything they ask for, it will be done for them by my Father in heaven" (Mt. 18:19).

* * *

Is it possible you haven't considered a difficult annoyance could be a spiritual attack? If so, how will you now handle it?

....

Melonie Janet's Musings

While walking in the illumination of the glorious gospel, you will find yourself at the mouth of dark, hidden caves. Afraid of the light, those inside may try to recede even farther into its depths for fear their deeds would be exposed. Their reluctance to turn and come toward the brilliant light will not prevail. Caught up in God's welcoming presence, they will be drawn into his majesty with a pull even stronger than a moth to a flame (Ps. 139:12).

....

Lana's Leadership Lines

Answering God's call involves risk-taking, something many believers are often reluctant to do. When God calls you to walk through a door of ministry opportunity, it is going to involve risk. You'll find yourself walking into the unknown, going places you've never been, and doing things you've never done before. These experiences require knowing the character of your Father in heaven, the power of the name of Jesus, and the equipping and guiding work of the Holy Spirit. Each risk opens new opportunities for growth and increase. Each victory makes trusting him easier.

As this experience in the Philippines shows, in faith we covered both the land and ourselves with the blood of Jesus. We partnered with the local leaders to bring light over darkness, trusting the blood of Jesus. We modeled and invited others into the actions that brought us together in partnership to expand his kingdom.

Leaders share responsibility. Leaders engage their authority in Christ in unity. Leaders represent truth in open, practical acts as an example and expectation of God's power. Be willing to do the same.

* * *

*Show me what to do and how to do it when I have
no clue, dear Lord Jesus.*

From Texas to Tanzania

Because He Said . . .

"Those who are planted in the house of the LORD shall flourish in the courts of our God. They shall still bear fruit in old age; they shall be fresh and flourishing, to declare that the LORD is upright" (Ps. 92:13-15, NKJV).

"With long life I will satisfy him and show him my salvation" (Ps. 91:16).

"God had planned something better for us so that only together with us would they be made perfect" (Heb. 11:40).

*   *   *

A friend introduced me to a nearly six-foot-tall, sixty-nine-year-old woman from Texas named Sue. She said Sue was a sharp teacher full of wisdom, just the kind of team partner I was looking for.

Sue's travels and ministry with us had a strong impact on the international women we served. They were shocked a woman of her age could travel like she does to bring the news of Jesus to the nations. Her story as a team member with Women With A Mission stretches from Japan, the Philippines, and then to Africa. Prior to joining us, she had been very active in ministry in Israel. Today, she is eighty-one and unequivocally informed me, "I will never quit!"

The following is Sue's story:

Sue's Story

Only a God of miracles can connect a team of women from all over the United States and unite them to be his voice and his hand extended to fulfill his will for the nations.

I was a housewife from Texas when I was asked to join Lana and her team on a trip to Tanzania, Africa. I had been on mission trips with Lana before and wondered each time if it would be my last trip. After all, I was retired. But I learned you never retire from serving the Lord. I am still teaching at age eighty-one. As many team members have realized, there is no age limit on the anointing.

The year was 2008, and we had been in other parts of Africa. Now we landed in Mwanza, Tanzania. We were meeting another team that was leading a coalition for native pastors from all over Africa. Many of these pastors were from small villages and had little in the eyes of the world, but they had a great hunger for the Word of God.

As we landed at an airport about two miles from town, we could see a small white building with a red roof boasting the words, "Welcome to Mwanza." As soon as we saw the building, our desire to minister to this new culture and country filled our hearts.

It wasn't long before we encountered our first challenge. As the luggage began appearing on the small conveyer belt, JoAnne's bag was missing. And so was mine. To report the lost luggage, we were taken to a tiny area with a desk and two chairs. Disappointed, we sat down and entered our names in a composition notebook. We could see there were already several pages of names. It certainly didn't give us much hope. The young clerk informed us, "Check back tomorrow."

I was grateful that I had at least packed a skirt and knit top in my carry-on bag. I had no idea this would be my uniform for four days. The first day I didn't mind, but when JoAnne showed up the second day in a borrowed beautiful blazer and skirt, I had to check my disappointment. My problem was that I am from Texas, and everything is bigger in Texas, including me. I knew no one would be my size, and therefore, I wouldn't be borrowing anything to wear soon.

By the third day, I wanted to announce to the whole assembly that my luggage was lost, and that was why I was wearing the same skirt and tennis shoes every day. The Lord dealt with me about my pride, and I knew he didn't want me to say anything. Why was it that I wanted them to know I had more clothes?

You've heard of having a pity party? I was tempted to hold a couple of those for short periods of time in the beginning. In Texas, we call them whimper shoot-outs. I knew God is bigger than any problem we have, and this wasn't a big problem after all. He gives more grace, and his ability in our inabilities shines through, even in the small things like what we have to wear. I submitted my emotions to the Holy Spirit's leading and didn't mention my lost luggage while teaching. I was surprised how something so small seemed to grant me a greater sense of freedom. He was showing me that it was not what I was wearing on the outside but what I had to give from the inside.

When JoAnne and I made our daily trip to the airport to check on luggage on the third afternoon, the young man showed us his composition notebook. "These are people who have lost luggage, and you will notice there are no checks beside their names showing they were found. I don't think your luggage is coming."

The Spirit of the Lord rose up within me, and I heard myself saying, "We are here on a mission from God. He knows where our luggage is, and he is going to dispatch his angels to find it, and our luggage is coming. I believe that. It will be here."

The next morning, we got the call. Luggage had arrived. Wow, God's angels had worked fast!

JoAnne and I were so happy; the driver of the car seemed to be exceedingly happy for us, too. Then when the people at the church heard, they, too, were celebrating that the lost luggage was found. It was a delight to see how overjoyed the employees at the airport were because our luggage had been found. Maybe the young man had told them we were expecting God's angels to find it, but there was still one disappointment. It was JoAnne's luggage that had arrived, not mine.

I turned to the young man and reminded him, "Mine is still on the way," and we left.

Grace, grace, God's grace. It was a little harder than the day before to once again put on the same skirt and tennis shoes, but I made it with his grace. Isn't it interesting how little things can be such a challenge to emotions at times?

One day later we got the call from the airport that my luggage had arrived. By now the whole village knew my bag had been lost and began rejoicing with the whole team. Everyone knew that if luggage was lost for four days, it wasn't found. It was a sign and wonder to them that our luggage had arrived. God's faithfulness lifted their faith, and we all gave him the glory.

The Power of Jesus' Name

Mission trips with a team of teachers seldom include a lovely tour through a country. Often, they have an intense focus on the work at hand, while praying into the expectation of miracles. Our heart's desire is to see the Holy Spirit do what only he can do—change lives. Sometimes it means going into the marketplace with open sewage running by our feet to be able to share the love of Jesus. Of course, there is always the ongoing prayer that the change in food will not become too big a challenge for our stomachs.

When you are a teacher, you prepare your message for a targeted audience for a specific day. On the mission field, teaching requires daily flexibility. The program could change in a few minutes, and you need to teach then instead of the next day, and possibly on a subject you hadn't planned for. It is common for schedules to change quickly, as on this trip when adjustments had to be made and speakers reassigned. But the incredible privilege and unexplainable joy we experienced was when the people stopped everything to listen. You could see their eyes light up with understanding. In all the changes of timing, content, and teachers, we celebrated our Holy Spirit–enabled unity as the meetings flowed in the Spirit of God.

Before leaving for this trip, Lana and Wendi had read an online teaching on Joshua 10. The sun and moon had stood still over Gibeon and Aijalon so the five kings could be captured in a cave at Makkedah. Overcoming the five Canaanite kings gave Joshua a great victory.

One evening after Pastor Wendi had finished speaking, she began her challenge to the congregation. A congregant sitting near the front starting crying and dramatically fell onto the floor. Several pastors ran to her side. They tried to bring comfort and deliverance from tormenting evil spirits. A local leader replaced Wendi at the pulpit as the distraction continued. After a few minutes, Lana and Wendi left the stage to help minister to the lady. They asked a few pastors to take her out the side door.

Lana leaned down and whispered into the woman's ear, "What is your name?"

The woman screamed out, "I am Makkedah."

Immediately, they knew the Holy Spirit had prepared them for this encounter. Since Lana had just studied this portion of Scripture, she knew what each name of the Canaanite cities meant. She demanded, "I know your name; I am calling you out!" She then commanded each of the names of the kings of Mekkedah. "In the name of Jesus, Mekkedah kings, come out!"

We watched them submit to the name of Jesus. He set the

woman completely free. What a sight to see the good news of Jesus come alive in front of our eyes once again.

Indescribable Joy

On these teams, you never know who is picking you up to speak at his church until the actual Sunday when they arrive. Often you climb into the car with the pastor, an interpreter, and a driver. During the conferences, I was drawn to an elderly, gray-haired pastor who had a beautiful smile and an obvious gentle spirit. I did not know who he was, but each day I would look to see if he was there. I began to pray for the Lord to bless this elderly man.

When we arrived at a village outside of Mwanza, to my delight I discovered I was in his church to minister. I felt as if I knew him already by the Spirit. I could tell he was loved and respected by his people, and that he loved the Lord with all his heart.

When he turned the meeting over to me, I could sense some restraint from the congregation. As always, I had my folder of notes, but somehow, I knew I shouldn't even open it. I shared with them how blessed I was at our previous meetings by the sweet spirit of this man of God, and how blessed they were to have him as their pastor.

Then, led by the Holy Spirit, I turned to where he was sitting on the platform and said, "I am ten thousand miles away from home this Sunday. Today, would you be my pastor and let me be part of your church family?"

You could feel the room change. All restraint was gone as he smiled broadly and nodded. The congregation started clapping. That day, I was one of them.

The folder of notes was never opened as the Holy Spirit began to lead the teaching. In the car on the way back to Mwanza, I apologized to my interpreter for not using the notes. He laughingly said, "It was no problem. All the interpreters want to interpret for you because you talk so slow and have that Texas drawl."

You can see why I am determined never to give up. The Bible refers to the feeling as indescribable joy. I have experienced this gracious gift from the Holy Spirit. I have tasted his indescribable joy.

A London Connection

When we make our plans, I believe God is smiling because he has his plans for our connections and collaborations, too. We ended our trip with a divine appointment in Heathrow Airport in London.

Lana had arranged for a van to take us to London to shop at Harrods, but there was a mix-up and the van did not arrive. Because there was no time to send for another one before we had to catch the next plane, JoAnne offered, "Let's go back into the airport to Starbucks, and I will buy the coffee."

The seating area in the airport kiosk was small. We took up three tables and were talking about our conferences and what God had done the past few days. At the table next to Lana was a well-dressed man reading a newspaper. He put his paper down and asked if we were Christians. We all turned our attention to him and answered, "Yes."

God's people in God's place at God's time. Harrods was out, and the Holy Spirit's connections became obvious.

The man explained that he was Jewish and worked for a Christian employer who was always trying to explain to him how the Gentiles were grafted into the Jewish roots, and that he still didn't understand it. "Could you explain it to me?"

Lana began to share Scriptures by getting out her Bible and showing him exactly where each one was found. The rest of us remained quietly praying for this divinely appointed meeting of a Jewish man and Christian women. We celebrated how the Holy Spirit never misses an opportunity to speak into an open heart.

About forty-five minutes later, his plane was announced. As we bid each other goodbye, we all knew his life was about to be transformed and began musing about how much this would bless his employer. The apostle Paul wrote in 1 Corinthians 3:6, "I planted the seed, Apollos watered it, but God has been making it grow." It was a synergistic upshift led by the Spirit of God. Who received the upshift this time? The inquisitive Jewish man. Does God still do miracles today? I respond in an unequivocal, "Yes!"

You, Too

"Greater is he that is in you, than he that is in the world" (1 John 4:4, KJV).

"Let us hold unswervingly to the hope we profess, for he who promised is faithful. And let us consider how we may spur one another on toward love and good deeds" (Heb. 10:23-24).

"Behold, I say to you, lift up your eyes and look at the fields, for they are already white for harvest!" (John 4:35, NKJV).

* * *

How is the Holy Spirit leading you to advance the kingdom of God? Have you discounted yourself due to age? If so, is it time to reconsider what the Holy Spirit is inspiring? How can you enter into the Holy Spirit's daily nudges for you, and how could this awareness affect your view of your career, family, or goals?

Melonie Janet's Musings
FINGERS
Fingers of truth readied upon the violin brings forth her sound as the bow of understanding moves across her path.

Lana's Leadership Lines
Sue has modeled leadership for the elderly and for those who follow her, yet she still affects the younger generations. Even

today, she teaches a Sunday school class for people ages twenty to ninety. Finishing well is something many in the Bible did not accomplish. Set your heart's goal to finish well.

* * *

Lord Jesus, I realize the apostle Paul prayed for the Ephesians that they would know what is the hope of their calling. Open my eyes to the Holy Spirit-initiated understanding. I look forward to your divine wisdom. Help me comprehend my value in the kingdom of God. I realize there is no age limit on the anointing. So I trust you are calling me and equipping me to bring life, energy, and passion to those around me, even to those of a drastically different age than my own. May there be intergenerational exchanges that plant and build strong lives filled with your Spirit.

Supernatural Languages

Because He Said . . .

"All of them were filled with the Holy Spirit and began to speak in other tongues as the Spirit enabled them" (Acts 2:4).

"Therefore, my brothers and sisters, be eager to prophesy, and do not forbid speaking in tongues" (1 Cor. 14:39).

* * *

When I served as an associate pastor, I would describe the gifts of the Spirit demonstrated during a church service as not always being obvious to attendees. We were casual in our expressions of what it meant to exhibit the spiritual gifts in 1 Corinthians 12–14. Therefore, the senior pastor encouraged sharing God's supernatural impartations in a natural-to-the-current-culture manner. After all, they are not merely a power gift we express on occasion at church but are to be part of our daily lives.

One Sunday, my husband and I were praying for the service while driving to church when it occurred to me that the Holy Spirit was asking me to give a message in front of the congregation on what the Bible refers to as the gift of tongues. When someone speaks in a Spirit-inspired, diverse, unlearned language, it is being supernaturally imparted for the purpose of blessing the hearers.

I had not spoken in my Holy Spirit–inspired language in front of the congregation in seven years, so the Holy Spirit's nudging was an intimidating request. The Bible also instructs that when a message in a supernatural language is given, someone with the gift of interpretation must interpret it. And, if there is no interpretation, the person speaking should interpret it. The risk was overwhelming. It seemed far too much pressure for me to obey the thought. There were so many ways to fail hearing God correctly or knowing what or how to bring the interpretation.

Over the years, when God has asked me to obey a direction, if I'm reluctant, he would graciously give me such a strong, passionate, heart-pounding push that I couldn't deny it was his intention. I began inwardly pleading for God to let me out of this. I wanted to be faithful to his leading, willing and obedient, but still I was reluctant. I petitioned, *If I must do this, please make it abundantly clear to the senior pastor.*

Speaking in Tongues

More than five hundred people had gathered in the congregation that Sunday, many of whom had never seen or heard anything like a word from God given in a supernatural language and interpretation. Would they be afraid? Would they want to leave the church because of confusion? How would I explain myself? What would happen if there was no interpretation? Could I ask one of the pastors or the audience if they had an interpretation?

I asked Pastor Dave if could speak to the congregation. He not said only yes, but stated he believed it was time for our congregation to begin to be exposed to the gifts of the Spirit. He said it was a good idea to give them a taste of what it looked and sounded like when in a gathering like ours.

Sure enough, at the end of the service, my heart was pounding, my thinking finally submitted to the push in the Spirit. Willingness began to supersede the fear.

When Pastor Dave gave me the nod, I stepped up to the microphone. I explained it would be a bit different for some of them. My attempts to get them ready to hear and receive a method of speaking they had never experienced before seemed feeble.

When I opened my mouth to speak, not only was there an abundance of spiritual words, but fervency of tone, hand motions, and all that goes with speaking, as if I understood what I was saying. When I finished, I realized it was likely I had frightened a few people and possibly confused others.

The other pastors were seated in the front row. In the pre-service meeting, I had shared with them my instruction and permission. "Listen up, guys. We will need a gift of interpretation this morning."

I looked down at them after a few minutes of speaking in my supernatural language for the interpretation. Their faces were blank, jaws dropped in surprise. No one moved to interpret. Now I had to listen for the interpretation myself to fulfill the biblical mandate.

I waited a few seconds, scanning the audience. No one spoke up or moved in their seats, so I proceeded to interpret what I believed God had been saying through the gift of tongues. It was encouragement for them regarding the character and love of God. When I finished, slinking out the side door seemed like a good exit. I had an unwelcome feeling of awkwardness.

Later, Pastor Dave reported one or two people left because of this demonstration. My heart sank. My obedience had created a conflict. I prayed, *Oh God, forgive me. I was sure you were asking me to do this. Help them forgive me and come back. Please fix it.*

At staff meeting the next week, Pastor Dave explained he believed the tongues and interpretation was the Holy Spirit speaking to us. "At the same time, no one realized the way God spoke through you with hand and body language. It just felt too out there for the congregation. Next time, don't deliver a message with such exuberance and body language. Hold it for the staff."

I wasn't upset with his evaluation or instructions. After all, he was the senior leader and responsible before God. My response was simply, "You draw the lines, and I will color within them."

When You Know, You Know

A couple weeks later, after church, I was serving at the information desk when a woman asked, "Do you remember the Sunday you spoke in tongues during service?"

"Of course," I responded.

Her serious facial expression caused me to think she was going to express upset or confusion. How severe was the negative reaction going to be? But instead, she told me a surprising story. "It was my first time visiting your church. I am from Fiji. I am preparing to bring my whole family to live in America. Did you realize you were speaking fluent Fijian?"

You can imagine my wide-eyed stare. I had no idea it was Fijian. In the past, I had spoken in tongues in a known language when a listening ear said I was speaking or singing in Arabic, Italian, Spanish, French, or a combination of others, but it was in smaller or private settings.

After the shock, I asked, "What about the interpretation? Did I get it correct?"

"You interpreted the general thought, encouraging the people about God's character and his deep, forgiving love," she said. "But it wasn't the exact words in Fijian. You were in the ballpark, though."

I was relieved that I had come close. Getting the interpretation correct had been my main concern. As I listened to the rest of her story, I asked God, *Why? There must be a reason. Why would you have me speak Fijian the first morning this Fijian lady came to church? What are you up to?*

It's a healthy principle in the Christian life to find out what the Holy Spirit has in his mind, and wise to join him. I wasn't about to miss this one. The experience was too unique to define as no more than a kind of supernatural manifestation that proved he's God.

As I listened, it occurred to me that the Holy Spirit was asking this woman to lead a team with me to Fiji in the near future.

"Why do you think God would do such a thing?" I asked, referring to my speaking her language.

She shook her head. "I have no idea."

I knew. How did I know? Only God knows how I knew. "I believe the Holy Spirit wants you and me to lead a team to Fiji. What do you think?"

"That's God, that's God," she said excitedly, her whole body responding. "I know this church, and the Fijian people would be a great match. I have been praying since that Sunday that we could take a team from here back to my country."

She was shocked I would make such an offer when we had just met. But when you know, you know. We prayed, we planned, and with twenty-eight other people, six months later we boarded a plane to taste our first adventure in Fiji. We ministered in churches, parks, schools, and a variety of settings. As you would expect, God was with us, transforming lives in each venue.

This one connection opened up three more trips to Fiji, collaborating with local churches and ministries on the island. I discovered the Holy Spirit was asking us to bring Fiji into our hearts for the greater expansion of the kingdom of God on its soil.

Who knew? Only God.

You, Too

"If you are willing and obedient, you will eat the good things of the land" (Isa. 1:19).

"When they heard this sound, a crowd came together in bewilderment, because each one heard their own language being spoken" (Acts 2:6).

* * *

Are you open to the Holy Spirit empowering you with the nuclear power of the supernatural gift of tongues? What is the Holy Spirit asking you to do in faith?

....

Melonie Janet's Musings

A sign and a wonder—who knew?
Not me. Likely, not you.
But there it was staring in our face;
a demonstration of his goodness,
a manifestation of his grace.
What now? What should we do?
Sit, bow, or walk on through?
In awe, we reverently worshiped.
How about you?

....

Lana's Leadership Lines

When speaking of ministry alignment, we must not only focus on aligning our actions with God's heart, but also our thoughts and willingness. When we do, we have more potential for aligning with one another in healthy, productive teamwork.

* * *

Heavenly Father, help me be obedient to the Holy Spirit's leading as well as in alignment with your appointed and anointed leaders without taking offense when there is a lack of understanding about what you are up to in the circumstance.

TRUE RELIGION

Because He Said . . .

*"Religion that God our Father accepts as pure and faultless is
this: to look after orphans and widows in their distress and
to keep oneself from being polluted by the world"*
(James 1:27).

* * *

Swaziland was desperate for life. AIDS had decimated its population
the year we arrived. Grandmas were raising their grandchildren
because the disease had taken their adult children. Due to the pandemic of AIDS, the local Assembly of God Bible school had trouble
getting year-round professors or teachers. Their creative idea was to
bring in teachers who were willing to teach a subject for a few weeks
at a time on a short-term basis. Lana was invited to teach the Old
Testament overview, and I (Janet) was invited to teach an introduction to the book of Hebrews.

Our team was met by the local missionaries who oversee the
church and school campus and a large, two-story brick home with
expansive lawns made for well-worn but adequate housing for short-
term guests like us and a long-term missionary couple. The ministry
that built the compound had a leadership failure that diminished
the funds for any upkeep of the building, but our room was more
than enough. The local hosts took us on a tour of the grounds,
which included a grassy hill between the home, the church, and the

Bible school. No streetlights or other lighted pathways were between them. We had morning and afternoon classes with women's conferences in the evening at the church.

Creatures of the Night

Our classrooms filled with expectant students diving into their Bible education. Watching Lana interact with the students while teaching the Old Testament was a joy for everyone. She was in her place of delight with the Lord and students. She absolutely loved teaching them. I enjoyed teaching, but for Lana it was different. Lana was a pacing mama when the tests were passed out. She was almost desperate for them to excel. She prayed for each test before she picked up her pen to grade. Her desire wasn't just for students to do well on a test, but that they absorb the life-giving principles she had taught for their future.

One dark night, we were to walk from the home to the church to speak at the women's ministry event. As we looked up at the black sky, I wondered aloud if we needed to watch for any wildlife. The young lady who was escorting us studied us with an odd expression. We thought she was probably pondering, *What's wrong with this crazy woman? Doesn't she know anything?*

Instead, she calmly commented, "Yes, cobras."

I haltingly responded, "Okay, and what should I do if I encounter one?"

Another one of those looks crossed the girl's face. With pursed lips and a slight head motion from right to left, she said in a firm tone, "Run."

Thank God we never saw a cobra. Flashlight in hand, with eyes darting in every direction, each night we crossed the lawns.

We needed to conquer other creatures, however. They weren't as dangerous as cobras. Nevertheless, our desire was to rid them from our presence in any way we could. Pointing at the wall, I said, "There it goes, Lana. See it? It's running between the bricks." It was the largest black cockroach we had ever seen, and we had seen some big ones. The ridges in the bricks became its escape as we madly banged the bricks, trying to squish that bug. Shoes in hand, we chased it around the walls, slapping at it as that swift creature dove into one of the grooves. If someone peeked in, we would have looked like we were crazy, running around the room with shoes in hand, banging on brick walls.

Then Lana had a brilliant idea. She grabbed her hairspray can from the bathroom—the kind that seals your hair hard as a rock. She valiantly chased that cockroach all around the room trying to drown it in hairspray—and it worked. Teamwork prevailed once again.

Bridge to Life

The next morning, we piled into the vans and traveled up a mountain to a rural area for another women's meeting. A woman who had a powerful testimony of being delivered from witchcraft had heard the voice of the Spirit of God leading her to minister to the grandmas and widows in the area. She had gathered them for us to speak to them.

Widows and grandmothers raising their grandchildren—and often another two or three sets of someone else's children—waited for us. The large outdoor cauldrons were boiling in preparation for our lunch while we sat on the lawn, sharing hearts. After lunch, we entered a small square building that had only a floor and walls. Grandmas and children, along with a few mothers with babies, sat on colorful patchwork blankets laid out on the floor.

It was time for the message. We barely had started when the children began to fidget and the babies began to cry, almost in unison. The moms attempted nursing them right away and settling down the younger ones, but to no avail. Lana and I moved over to the side of the room where no one else could hear. We took authority against any evil spirits that would try to agitate the

Tank in Afghanistan

Afghanistan women dancing

Luggage carriers in India

Military and team in Sri Lanka

Widow relief in Sri Lanka

*Nora and Romeo Corpuz
with Lana in the Philippines*

*Dressed in our saris
in India*

Samuel and Pratiba Stephens in India

Sandy in Punjab, India

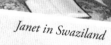

Janet in Swaziland

*Janet baptizing
in China*

Lana's team in Uganda with Pastor Godfrey Saazi

Pat Kempf and team in Brazil

Lana and Janet praying for pastors

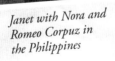

Janet with Nora and Romeo Corpuz in the Philippines

Austrailia CHOGM Event

children and disrupt our time with the women.

It was as if a conductor had taken his baton and ordered a moment of silence, then with his baton in the air, reengaged the music. Immediately, peace and quiet prevailed. The message started once more, and we had everyone's attention. After a short period of time, the ruckus would start up again. We repeatedly took our authority over the spirits, and again the room settled down until the enemy was thoroughly defeated. Jesus' lordship made the way for peace to remain.

Those who had not known the Lord joyfully received him that day. Those who did know him were greatly encouraged with his mercy and hope. The women were full of questions, which we loved answering. We felt like a bridge to life when discouragement could have won the day. Hopelessness and despair were washed away. It was a day of God bringing hope with a validation of their hard work and loving hearts, as seen by the Holy Spirit himself.

Even though they were desperately in need while raising their grandchildren, by the time we left, the women were clapping and singing. The Holy Spirit had strengthened their resolve. He had met them in an extraordinary way. Laughter flowed through the room, and before long, they had gotten up from the floor and one by one danced through the room for a few minutes, sharing their dance moves with one another. Then another would join until we all found ourselves celebrating together in dance.

You, Too

"Because of this oath, Jesus has become the guarantor of a better covenant" (Heb. 7:22).

"But in fact the ministry Jesus has received is as superior to theirs as the covenant of which he is mediator is superior to the old one, since the new covenant is established on better promises" *(Heb. 8:6).*

* * *

Who around you is going through a hard time and is in great need of perseverance? Who needs the hope of a "better covenant" than the one they are currently experiencing?

....

Melonie Janet's Musings

Love is strong in confidence and quieted in peace.

Love knows Almighty God is Lord of all and gives the helpless increase.

Love's ways are caring.

Love's manner is both forceful and tender.

Love's reward can always be found in her God who daily commends her.

....

Lana's Leadership Lines

The word *better* is used throughout the book of Hebrews—thirteen times, to be exact. Its application is to describe the New Covenant in relation to the Old Covenant. Scholars say its purpose was to exhort Christians to persevere in the face of persecution. Certainly, the students attending the Bible college as well as the grandmothers, widows, and orphans in Swaziland understood what it means to persevere through troubling times. Can you relate?

The better covenant Jesus gave us comforts and motivates us

to love and obey God. The book of Hebrews stimulates us to love one another with good deeds—living in ways that demonstrate faith, obedience, thankfulness, reverence, and love. It challenges us to hold fast to the confession of our hope without wavering, for he who promised is faithful; and consider how to stimulate one another in love and good deeds (Heb. 10:23-24). It's all about relationship with God and with people. His love compels us to reach not only into others' lives, but also to find ways to help meet practical needs.

* * *

Dear heavenly Father and Lord Jesus, I am trusting the Holy Spirit to stimulate me to live according to the "better covenant." Extend your love and fulfill your purpose for my life. Help me demonstrate faith, obedience, thankfulness, and reverence, and may the challenges purify my soul.

ONE IS WORTH IT

Because He Said . . .

"'For my thoughts are not your thoughts, neither are your ways my ways,' declares the LORD. 'As the heavens are higher than the earth, so are my ways higher than your ways and my thoughts than your thoughts'" (Isa. 55:8-9).

* * *

In *Set My Heart on Fire*, Lee Grady writes, "Be willing to go to out-of-the-way places. God told the evangelist Philip to leave the exciting revival meetings in Samaria and go to a remote place on a desert road (Acts 8:26). His obedience led to the conversion of a eunuch from Ethiopia, who then planted the gospel in that nation. Because we think spiritual impact is measured by large crowds, we often neglect one-on-one conversations. Sometimes the most strategic ministry moments involve just one spiritually desperate individual."

Have you noticed how the Holy Spirit's schedule often doesn't seem to take our schedules into consideration? He is constantly stretching us beyond our strength and comfort zones, so it is evident that he is the power in us that spreads the gospel message. This was never more apparent than the time that I was preparing to fly home on an international flight in the midst of an especially exhausting mission trip with Lana, Merrily, and Shirani in Sri Lanka.

One-on-One Connection

Tired of traveling, I was aching for comfort and longing for my own bed and pillow, when I received a surprise email from my husband and brother-in-law. They had found a bargain upgrade to business class for the next four-hour leg of my trip. Deep appreciation filled my soul. I had just spent several days sitting in very uncomfortable straight-backed, hard plastic chairs. I could already imagine myself lying down on the plane, resting my aching body. Sure enough, as I boarded the airplane, I saw that a roomy, lie-flat seat was to be mine. It was directly across from Lana and Merrily. Happily, I would only have one neighbor.

I was nestled into my luxurious seat when a young teenage girl sat next to me. I wanted to be polite by at least saying hello. She warmly answered, and as we waited for the flight to take off, she began some light chitchat, with simple relational questions. I realized this was not a typical teenager. Certainly, she was not only bright, but also honestly curious about my lifestyle, especially my worldview.

I soon discovered our age difference was fifty-five years. It is not uncommon for a younger person to have little or no interest in talking to someone so much older than themselves. If there is a conversation, it tends to be more about their interests, such as movies, school, or a love life. Most teenagers soon tire of the senior citizen next to them on an airplane and return to their cell phones and other devices. I cherish my alone time, too, but God had a different plan.

The more we shared, the more I realized this was a God-ordained appointment. The girl's Muslim religion was drastically different from my very personal relationship with Jesus. We spent at least two hours sharing life experiences about family, countries, education, dreams, and goals before I decided it was time to tell her that I was a believer and follower of Jesus.

I learned that this young lady was going home on a school

break, but she was also on her own journey of faith. When she arrived home, she would be living in a small community with rigid rules that would have precluded us from ever meeting. But now, thirty thousand feet above God's beautiful earth, we had the freedom to speak freely.

As the flight attendant passed by, she leaned over and whispered something to the young woman in her own language. I asked if I could know what she had said. "Yes," the girl replied. "The flight attendant said, 'I think you have found a lifetime friend.'"

Our lunch was served, and we took a break to quietly eat. I wondered if she would don her earphones as most young people would to signal the end of our conversation. But, no. After lunch, she continued to ask questions about my world and my eternal perspective of life. We talked about how we could each see the value of life here and what eternity could be. We shared deep beliefs regarding God's heart for humanity.

I was fully engaged in what is often referred to as missional listening, which means I was both listening to her and the Holy Spirit at the same time. I was peaceful and felt gently led by the Spirit, often finding bridges of similarity, or even the same principle. For the first time in her life, she was hearing about God's love and his desire that not one perish. Coming from belief systems and worldviews that were worlds apart, we found ourselves forging a sweet new friendship, sharing our hearts.

As wisely as I could follow the leading of the Holy Spirit, we talked over three hours. The girl seemed curious and continued to share her own faith with me. It was an honor to have spent that time with her. It brings such gratefulness to my soul when I think about that meeting. Then, if that weren't enough, she sent me the following email when I got home:

> Hi! This is _____, the girl on the plane. As you may have already guessed I have already arrived in my home

country, thank God (I most certainly did not miss the desert heat). I'm writing this email to thank you for sharing so much of your wisdom with this sixteen-year-old, inexperienced high school junior. As I've already told you, I find your faith and continuing curiosity with the world's wonders something to truly be in awe of. One day I wish to have a faith as unwavering as yours, because I think to believe in something with all your heart without ever having seen it makes a beautiful soul (and with the conversation we had on the plane, I know how beautiful yours is). You've shared many of your life stories with me, and for that I'm truly thankful to have been able to simply sit and listen. I hope all went well in the country you were ministering in. I hope you've helped heal and touch the lives of those people as you have with me.

A heart as kind and warm as yours has brightened the lives of many, including mine. I now thank God for letting our paths cross on that Friday, because it is an encounter I will cherish forever in my memories. I've made an indelible friend, and I hope you think the same of me. May God bless you on the rest of your journeys, whether that be on this life or after.

You, Too

"What do you think? If a man owns a hundred sheep, and one of them wanders away, will he not leave the ninety-nine on the hills and go to look for the one that wandered off? And if he finds it, truly I tell you, he is happier about that one sheep than about the ninety-nine that did not wander off" (Matt. 18:12-13).

* * *

Are you concerned about being completely open to Holy Spirit–led interactions with those of drastically different faiths than your own? What would you consider the most difficult areas to face?

....

Melonie Janet's Musings

Each person is precious, for each life Jesus died.
Could there be a greater privilege than being
Father's oracle to his creation, humankind?
What do I perceive when I look at the sea of humanity?
What would I consider Father's highest honor?
How about being invited to craft with the Master Craftsman?
Am I ready to highly esteem that which he conferred worthy of
    honor, all Jesus died to redeem? Holy Spirit, as I think about
    these questions, I ask you to fill the gaps I perceive.

....

Lana's Leadership Lines

We can discount God-led moments as coincidence. We can criticize our efforts. But when we keep our heart motives genuine, his ability to transcend differences is astounding.

Our presence makes a difference, whether we say a few words or spend hours with someone. Be sensitive to the Holy Spirit at all times. Become aware that some seemingly unimportant coincidences are divine appointments that can change someone's eternal destination.

* * *

Holy Spirit, help me be aware when there is an open heart nearby.
Lead me in my conversations, and grant me the sincerity and
integrity to extend your merciful love, Jesus.

OUTRAGEOUS FAITH

Because He Said . . .

"Let us not become weary in doing good, for at the proper time we will reap a harvest if we do not give up"
(Gal. 6:9).

* * *

I was sitting in the back of an audience of probably 3,500 people, listening to Jane Hansen Hoyt, president of Aglow International, open the session. I heard my name announced as the new evangelism director. That signaled the beginning of the Office of Evangelism in the Transformation Department of Aglow International, and the beginning of many experiences of outrageous faith.

Connections of the Spirit

At lunchtime, Ines, the Brazilian leader of Aglow, asked to speak with me. "I have been reaching out to a small group of women in Sao Paolo near my home. Would you consider bringing a team to help them learn a sewing skill?"

She began to share her heart for these impoverished women who provided for their families through prostitution. She wanted to help them find a way out of their predicament and, of course, see them become sisters in the Lord. As I listened, I silently petitioned, *Is this your idea, Lord?* I couldn't deny the firm *yes* in my mind as the Holy Spirit spoke to my heart.

My immediate, prayerful thought back to him was, *Then you have to send me someone who specializes in sewing and someone who helps start small businesses.*

Ines and I looked at the calendar and made our preliminary plans for a team to come in the following year. Soon after, Doreen approached me. "I live in Newfoundland and own a sewing and fabric business. Can you use me in the Evangelism Department?"

My internal grin broadened. "Yes. Can you be in Brazil in May?"

"Yes," was her swift answer.

I silently reminded the Holy Spirit, *Now, I need someone who can teach how to start and maintain a small business.* Pat Kempf, who owned her own business, approached me next. And, of course, she was an accomplished seamstress.

"Pat, could you teach sewing and help the women learn how to start their business?" I asked.

You know her answer was yes. Pat's friend, Sheri, who was an entrepreneur in a small business, had taught Pat how to make jewelry. Sheri wanted to come, too, and teach jewelry making as well as how to start a business. Next, Pam joined us, and she already had a jewelry-making business. Doreen brought a friend from Newfoundland to help with the training. In a matter of a few months, the team was ready. I know the Holy Spirit isn't always that obvious in timing. But he had made it clear these were his connections for Aglow Brazil, to be able to reach these moms.

Ines' friend asked her English-speaking daughter to serve as our interpreter. A recovering addict with perfect English, the girl's response was, "No way. I don't want to interpret for some old religious women."

But her mother prevailed, and our team grew by one more. This woman's daughter not only interpreted the skills we wanted to teach, but she also interpreted the daily devotions and sermons at the end of each training time.

The Holy Spirit never misses an opportunity to transform a life when the person is open and willing to come to him. Not only did our precious interpreter receive Jesus, but she is now married with two children, and completely delivered from her past.

The testimonies of God's redemptive, transformative presence were glorious for everyone who attended. The women learned a new skill in sewing, jewelry making, and how to start a small business, and their families became our brothers and sisters in the Lord. This was the beginning of many outreaches into Brazil for evangelism and discipleship under Pat's leadership, collaborating with Ines, Martha, and others. The result was always the same: new believers, new skills, and new transformations in families.

No Problem for God

After a few years, I was asked to return to Brazil with Pat. She and Ines were planning an outreach in Sao Paolo for the young moms whose kids attended a special needs school. I reminded Pat that we both needed new Brazilian visas, but she was sure hers didn't expire until the following year. I made my appointment at the Brazilian embassy in Los Angeles for that July to get a new one. In the meantime, Pat discovered I was right—her visa had expired.

It may sound ridiculous, but the location for obtaining a visa if you live in Montana like Pat was Los Angeles, California. Pat would need an appointment to turn in her paperwork. This was the evening of July 14, and we were scheduled to fly out on August 4. She began praying in the Spirit.

Pat began to think outside the box. Maybe I could turn in her paperwork at the same time I had my appointment? It could be possible if she filled out her visa application, overnighted her passport to me with a picture, and paid a fee. But she would have to set up her own appointment at the same time I had mine.

Unfortunately, the first appointment available was August 13. The online instructions said to send an emergency email if an earlier appointment was needed, so she tried that. While she waited for a response, Pat got a certified cashier's check for the visa fee and a new passport picture, and overnighted everything to me.

We knew our heavenly Father would work it out, but we still had nagging concerns. When the time came for my appointment, she still hadn't heard back from the embassy. I took Pat's paperwork with me, hoping they would accept it. They refused.

It was a little scary thinking of Pat flying to Brazil with an expired visa. She had confidence in God that he would come through, and it was too late to cancel the trip. There was no one else on the team who could teach quilting like we had planned. So she kept working on the projects, preparing to go.

Finally, after three emails to the emergency email address, she received a reply that said her circumstances did not constitute an emergency. We kept praying.

I asked my husband, Tom, to drive me to Los Angeles to the Brazilian consulate to pick up my visa. We thought we had left home in plenty of time for heavy traffic. And yet, as we were getting close, it looked like we wouldn't make the appointment due to congested streets. The consulate made no exceptions for late arrivals. We were praying for God's intervention, and I was hopeful they would, somehow, miraculously accept Pat's packet this time.

Meanwhile, Pat had been going online every few minutes for several hours, trying to get an appointment that coincided with my picking up my visa. She was hoping one would be canceled, and she could swoop in and claim it. As Tom and I got closer to the Brazilian office, I kept Pat on the cell phone, while she kept checking the website.

Just as we drove into the underground parking lot, Pat yelled, "I've got an appointment! At noon today!"

I looked at the clock in the car. It was 11:50 a.m.

I told her to text her confirmation number. Then I threw open the car door and began to run. As I entered the building, I had to enter my appointment number in the kiosk before going to the window. I walked into the room in time to hear my name and window number being announced. As I was receiving my completed visa, I heard Pat's number and name being announced.

Tom had gotten Pat's confirmation number, entered it into the kiosk, and was at that moment walking into the room. I signaled for him to go to the window and give them Pat's packet. He turned in all the documents, and they said it would be processed in a week. With seconds to spare, I had picked up mine and turned in hers. My timing for arrival had been planned by the Holy Spirit.

In the week between turning in Pat's passport and picking up the visa, we found out there was no way I could send everything to Pat and have her get it before she would need to be at the airport in Billings. Instead, when I picked up Pat's passport, I took a picture of the new visa and emailed it to her.

Pat left for the airport with just a picture of her passport and new visa. Not only would it be a miracle if the airline attendant allowed her to board the plane to Chicago, but Pat also would have to have the actual passport and visa in hand in order to board the plane for Brazil.

No problem.

More Miracles to Come

I was traveling to Brazil with team member Lynn, and we had selected a flight that would go through O'Hare International. Why did we choose to go through Chicago when it meant we would be on the plane for hours more? Now we can see the Holy Spirit's wisdom in the planning when we had no idea it was him. Our going through Chicago was critical.

In international travel, you must show your passport not only before you get on the plane to the final destination, but also at your first flight. I knew Pat had faith that she would get on that plane in Billings, even if the Holy Spirit had to blind them to the fact that she did not have proper paperwork. Pat never doubted that God was going to do a miracle. Sure enough, he did. They let her on the plane with copies of her proper documents.

But Pat's plane was delayed. She was not going to arrive in time to catch her connecting flight to Brazil—and I had her visa and passport. Lynn and I got in the airline information line to see what might be worked out. At least twenty people stood ahead of us. And our flight, which was different from Pat's, was being announced for boarding.

As a man with an airline logo on his shirt walked past us, I grabbed his attention and said, "Sir, it's an emergency. We have a problem with an incoming late flight."

He stopped and listened. After I shared a short version of the story about Pat and her visa, he smiled. "You're in luck. I am working that flight to Sao Paolo and am headed to that gate now. If her flight lands in the next fifteen minutes, I will take care of her and make sure she gets on the next flight."

I immediately texted Pat, whose flight from Billings was just landing: "Ask the stewardess to put you up front, explain why, and have your carry-on with you. When you get off, run as fast as you can to the gate. The agent will meet you and get you on a flight."

We needed to leave for our flight and hadn't heard back from Pat. We asked God to work a miracle. As soon as we saw Pat come running around the corner of the terminal, Lynn and I rushed to the information desk as the agent was ready to leave and shouted, "We've got her, we've got her! Here are her documents."

He replied, "Okay. Get to your flight, and I will take care of her."

Roadblock or Gift?

With deep breaths and thankful hearts, Lynn and I ran to our departure gate. Our heart rates finally settled down as we searched for our seats. Our seats had been changed, and Lynn was stuck in an uncomfortable middle seat between two hefty gentlemen. Just then a crew member announced that passengers could pay $500 for an upgrade to business class. Although it seemed extravagant, Lynn and I hurried off the plane to the agent selling the seats. It was the same agent who had helped us earlier.

"I put your friend in a lounge room, got her luggage off-loaded, and booked her on the next flight out after yours," he said.

Thanking him profusely, we could hear him whisper to the agent taking our credit cards, "Charge them $200."

Thank God for a restful trip to Brazil. Upon arrival, we were taken to our lodgings around 9 a.m. And when do you think Pat arrived? Midnight that same night.

No one but our heavenly Father, via the Holy Spirit, could have provided for us in such a timely manner. We mere minutes away at each turn when plans could have fallen apart. Lynn and I wondered what dynamic experience we were going to have, since he made it so clear it was his idea to be in Brazil.

The One Lost Sheep

Our meeting room at the school facility was barely large enough to fit a couple of tables and supplies, but Ines, Martha, and Pat managed to train the moms how to sew and make quilted purses. For five days, we all helped iron fabric and measure patterns. Every morning, I began with a ten-minute devotion regarding God's love, Jesus' forgiveness, and his desire to rescue our eternal lives. By the end of the week, the women proudly finished their colorful purses.

When I gave the last message about his love rescuing their hearts, the moms not only wanted to say prayers for forgiveness and salvation, but were so excited that they began jumping up and down. Hugs, and hugs again, laughter, dancing, and beautiful friendships were born from our week together. The head of the school attended the session on the last day of sewing and celebration. She, too, was ready to pray with us for her eternal life to be born from above.

The trip did not lead to thousands coming to salvation. I don't remember if there were more than two healings. Yet the Lord had gone to incredible lengths to get us there. We might consider this result surprisingly small. But from God's point of view, the lives touched were priceless and well worth it all.

You, Too

"Look at the birds of the air; they do not sow or reap or store away in barns, and yet your heavenly Father feeds them. Are you not much more valuable than they?"
(Matt. 6:26).

"For I am not ashamed of the gospel of Christ, for it is the power of God to salvation for everyone who believes, for the Jew first and also for the Greek. For in it the righteousness of God is revealed from faith to faith, as it is written, 'The just shall live by faith'"
(Rom. 1:16-17, NKJV).

* * *

Are there areas in your life where the Spirit of the Lord is whispering, *Don't give up?* Is it possible they could be fulfilled in an entirely different way than your original requests?

Melonie Janet's Musings

There are times to let go and times to lean in. How wonderful to know that God's relationship with us is so intimate, his details never fail. As our omnipotent Father and creator of the universe, he is able to arrange people and situations to accomplish his will. What is impossible with man is now possible. His miracles can be cliff-hangers for sure, but what an exciting story as we hang on and endure.

....

Lana's Leadership Lines

Discerning God's leading often requires outrageous faith. Perseverance is a quality of the Holy Spirit. God makes a way when there is no way. Where God guides, he provides. He rewards those who earnestly seek him.

* * *

Father God, I realize we all have a measure of faith. But today I am asking you to help me grow from faith to faith, strength to strength, and glory to glory, and experience the outrageous faith that comes from the spiritual gift of faith.

BE A VOICE

Because He Said . . .

"Then I heard the voice of the Lord saying, 'Whom shall I send? And who will go for us?' And I said, 'Here am I. Send me!'" (Isa. 6:8).

"See, I have engraved you on the palms of my hands; your walls are ever before me" (Isa. 49:16).

* * *

Of all the nations God has sent me to, the Philippines has remained at the top of the list. It was there where I first heard God's voice telling me that he would be sending me to be a voice, along with other women, to women of many nations. In the history of Women With A Mission, I have led or sent more teams to the Philippine Islands than any other place on earth. Team member JoAnne has been there several times.

JoAnne has mentored me for twenty-four years in ministry as a friend, advisor, and board member. A former regional director of Aglow International, she is a groundbreaker and pioneer, having served her state and local church as an advisor, teacher, inspirational leader, and business leader. Her longevity in the business world as well as ministry in the Christian community have enabled her to empower God's people to move from the church into the market-place with influence and excellence.

JoAnne travels globally to train and inspire pastors and people of all ages. People are inspired and released into their destiny as she ministers in the gifts of wisdom, prophecy, and words of knowledge. Her gifts of teaching and storytelling are evident in her story of one special trip to the Philippines.

*   *   *

The following is JoAnne's story:

The Eye of the Storm

I was scheduled to speak in Manila to a group of Christian pastors and leaders. How we ever got there, I will never know. There were no road signs—only a maze of littered and dusty gravel roads with many twists and turns. When we arrived an hour later, the driver lifted his hands in praise. "This is it!" he exclaimed, thanking God he had found it.

Inside the church building, a roomful of pastors and leaders waited with great anticipation. I, on the other hand, was more than a little scared. And yet I also sensed a sacred moment was about to happen. I had never spoken to a group of foreign pastors about the hazards of religious mindsets versus the safety of being kingdom-minded. The message was hard because it would require them to tear down the religious walls they had erected around their churches. The Holy Spirit was the only one who could compel them to change.

Lana's words sizzled like a hot branding iron in my mind. "Remember, English is their second language. Don't use Western clichés. Speak slowly. If you see blank stares, repeat what you just said in another way, or ask them if they understood."

When I began speaking, I became more confident. The pastors appeared to be tracking with me. They laughed and nodded in all the right places. Feeling supercharged, I challenged them to look for God's new assignments.

"No longer can you shelter yourself within the walls of your church," I declared. "Look beyond the city gates, and be a kingdom sound in your nation. It was a holy shout that caused the walls of Jericho to crumble. It was a holy shout from Gideon that destroyed the enemy. In the same manner, shout out to the Filipino warriors that you are fully equipped for victory against your enemy, not because you have a formula but because God is with you and within you."

And then the Holy Spirit downloaded this thought: *Share your dream about sound.*

But, Lord, they won't understand, I argued.

His prodding was sharper this time. (A little advice here—don't argue with God.) And so, I obeyed.

"Last month, on October 5," I began, "I had a dream. I was caught in a violent storm. Debris was flying everywhere, and the howling wind twisted and contorted my body until it felt like my skin was about to rip off. Suddenly, an angel pulled me out of the chaotic whirlwind and dropped me into the very eye of the storm. Although I could still hear the roar of the storm, nothing but peace could touch me. It felt good to be at rest. And then I heard the angel shout, 'JoAnne! Awake! Arise!'

"Immediately, I sensed a seamless robe, alive with color and movement, drop upon my shoulders. When I opened my eyes, I noticed the digital clock marking the time as 4:40 a.m. The number 440 is significant in the world of sound. It's the universal concert pitch of the A note. Interestingly, songs tuned to 440 hertz are known to influence the brain toward conflict and unrest. I wondered if the whirlwind in my dream symbolized a world in chaos. But according to my dream, I understood that we don't have to live there. God provides a place for us in the very center of his will. Therefore, when the enemy stirs up bedlam, we can war from that place of calm and rest with an unshakable voice of authority, power, and peace."

Suddenly, a young man jumped out of his seat and called out, "Reverend JoAnne, God spoke to me, too."

Waving a small book in his hand, he ran to me and opened his journal to the page marked October 5, 2007. On that very day at 4:40 a.m.—the same date and time of my dream—God asked him if he would be willing to be God's voice, his sound to the Filipino people. To go where God sent him, to speak what the Holy Spirit told him to say, and to love the way God loves. Many of the same words I had heard from God that day were written in his journal.

The young man continued, "I made a contract with God right then and signed my name to make it official. And then I heard the Lord say, *I am sending a witness to confirm to you everything I have said to you.*" By faith, the young man had drawn another line underneath his name for that witness. "And here you are!" he exclaimed. "Will you sign your name on this line?"

As I wrote my name on the dotted line, the room exploded with loud praises to God. Instantly, the Holy Spirit began to drop mantles of authority and new assignments upon the pastors' shoulders. It was a hallelujah moment and an amazing breakthrough. For years, the pastors had told me that they had relied on foreigners to prophesy, teach, and hear from God for their nation. On this day, they themselves had been freshly anointed to carry God's unconditional love and supernatural power to their people.

God had sent a woman from Alaska to the barrios of Manila to witness this sacred moment.

Tattooed on His Hand

The next day, our team squeezed into a big van and headed to the province of Bulacan. It was a harrowing ride. From every direction, hundreds of speeding jeepneys and supply trucks honked warnings, sucking the air around our van as they flew by. The actual mileage from Manila to Bulacan is only fifteen miles. However, due to the enormous size of Manila and creeping traffic, it took us one hour and twenty minutes.

On our very first night of meetings, the tone was set. Personal prayer continued well into the night. Spines moved back into alignment, and legs grew straight before our eyes. Deaf ears opened, and goiters dissolved. Pockets of joy and laughter broke out whenever another person experienced a miracle. One man who had a dense tumor the size of an orange came forward for prayer, but nothing happened. But he didn't give up. Throughout the two-day event, he continued to ask people to lay hands on the tumor. By the end of the conference, it had become a flat spot of wrinkled skin.

Traditionally, international speakers are asked to eat with the pastors and leaders. I was excited because I thought it meant I wouldn't be eating fried fish and white rice again. Maybe there would be a small piece of chicken. Sitting down at the long, wooden table, I stared into a steaming bowl of fish eye soup. Glassy eyeballs stared up at me through the pasty gray broth that looked like last night's dishwater.

It freaked me out. I didn't care that fish eyeballs were considered a tasty delicacy. I wanted out of there. The longer those eyeballs stared at me, the less I cared who I might offend.

Lord, help me! I prayed.

Just then Janet came rushing over. "JoAnne, they need someone to teach the children. Can you come with me right now? They're waiting."

Thank you, Lord, for rescuing me! I breathed silently, gave my apologies to the pastors, and ran with Janet to meet the children.

Neither of us had teaching for children in our ministry toolkits. We prayed. The thought of thirty young children staring, waiting for me to do something, was almost as unsettling as those fish eyes staring up at me.

From a distance, we could see the children waiting under a huge shade tree. We were desperate. We prayed some more. And then a word popped into my thoughts. "Janet, I've got it—tattooed!"

She looked at me strangely. "You lead—I'll follow."

We greeted the children, introduced ourselves, and then asked, "What's your favorite Sunday school song?"

"Zacchaeus," they said in unison.

"Do you mean the short man who climbed into a sycamore tree to see Jesus?"

"Yes."

The children taught us the song, with all the hand motions. They'd giggle when we got it all wrong. Finally, after the third or fourth time, we knew the lyrics and were able to follow their hand motions.

"Do you think Jesus forgot about Zacchaeus?" I asked.

They shook their heads.

"Why not?"

"Because they were good friends. Jesus even went to his house."

"Have you ever felt Jesus forgot about you?"

Some of the children said yes, others weren't sure, and some were certain God wouldn't remember their name. And he certainly hadn't come to their house for a visit. Opening my Bible, I read Isaiah 49:16 and explained how God would never forget them because their names and their lives were tattooed on the palm of his hand.

Being inspired, I said, "Let's pretend our hands are the hands of God. Would you like to write your name on God's hand?"

The children lined up with anticipation. After the first signature, we realized we needed another plan because our sweaty palms washed away the ink in seconds. Janet quickly pulled out two sheets of paper and drew a large right and left hand. As each child signed their name, we prayed for their future. We could sense the atmosphere growing thicker with God's presence. When the last child stepped forward, he found an empty spot in the middle of the right hand and signed his full name in big, bold block letters. Just as Paul did to Timothy, we placed our hands on his head and stirred up the spiritual gifts within him, sensing God had already anointed him for service.

That evening, the same nine-year-old boy delivered an unfiltered prophecy to the people. When he walked onto the platform, all eyes turned to watch. In a strong voice, he called the people to arise and be a voice for the kingdom of God. He told them to breathe in God's peace so they would be strong in battle against the enemy.

In closing, we exhorted everyone present to pick up the spiritual tools God was handing out to do the new and expanded work in their country. This was an important message for the Filipino people, as well as for the WWAM team. Through our obedience, we had become a catalyst for God to change the mindsets of these amazing, passionate people.

The spontaneous teaching on Isaiah 49:16 with the children had been so well received and demonstrated, we decided to teach it at a women's conference in Baguio City. Again, we were astounded by the response. Once the women realized God knew their name and had engraved it personally on the palm of his hand, they were ready to hear more. They were amazed when they heard he knew everything about them, and despite it all, he still wanted to help them fulfill their destiny.

They had stories they couldn't tell in church. Secrets they couldn't share. Scars they couldn't reveal. Places in the soul they'd never gone to because it didn't feel safe. The teaching helped them reconnect back to God's original plan. They understood the Holy Spirit would go the distance with them. He was someone they could trust.

When the call went out for them to sign their names on the two symbolic hands of God outlined on the six-foot-long blackboard, hundreds of women jumped out of their seats and ran—not walked— to make their mark. When the outlines were filled, they started writing all over the blackboard. And when the blackboard was filled, they wrote their names on the wooden frame around the board.

The women believed in God's unconditional love for them. They felt empowered to build his kingdom of love in their nation. It was a sacred, unforgettable moment. This mission trip helped me understand that the impact of our team was not based upon our gifts or skill level, but the deep love and trust of the Father.

You, Too

"'Am I only a God nearby,' declares the LORD, 'and not a God far away? Who can hide in secret places so that I cannot see them?' declares the LORD. 'Do I not fill heaven and earth?'"
(Jer. 23:23-24).

* * *

What can you envision changing when you fully submit your voice to the Holy Spirit? How would that impact your everyday life? Who does God love that he wants to send you to? Will you be willing to go?

Melonie Janet's Musings
GOD TO GOD AGAIN

We, the statement of God's enduring mercy, are endeavoring to know his Word and follow his ways. Ah yes, not only to be in the heart of God, a part of his very self, but to operate in his ways so we become the heartbeat and outraying of the Deity in every circumstance and situation. Then we, the collective blending of his voice, create a full circle as a rainbow when seen from the air—from God to God again.

Lana's Leadership Lines

Who among us can dare to say we understand the love of God so fully that we trust him in every circumstance, listen, and obey his voice? We all have moments of doubt, but his love and faithfulness remain steady.

* * *

*Lord, I want to build your kingdom by trusting your heart
for all generations. Therefore, I ask you to help me make your
mark on our world. Thank you, Lord, for filling the whole earth
with your love. Thank you for helping me follow love, to give it
authority in my life so I might connect others to you. Help me
value people—to see people as you see them. I pray my
life will display your glory. Amen.*

Teamwork in Punjab

Because He Said . . .

*"The Spirit of the Lord is on me, because he has anointed me
to proclaim good news to the poor. He has sent me to
proclaim freedom for the prisoners and recovery of sight for
the blind, to set the oppressed free" (Luke 4:18).*

"Love never fails" (1 Cor. 13:8).

*"Who shall separate us from the love of Christ? Shall trouble
or hardship or persecution or famine or nakedness or danger
or sword?" (Rom. 8:35).*

* * *

India is both intriguing and challenging. With its vast landmass, multiple people groups, colorful landscapes, and differing traditions, it is hard to wrap your head around its kaleidoscopic identity.

The Delhi airport parking lot is shocking for novice travelers. It was for me (Janet). Our carts were piled high with luggage. The team darted through the shoving crowds, making their way to their transports. I had never experienced such aggressive human traffic. My attempts at politeness weren't getting me two inches forward. The pressing crowd seemed bent on getting ahead with cold, determined stares. Carts slamming into one another in front of me gave no pathway to join the rest of the team waiting at the van.

Perplexed, I scanned the parking lot for Lana.

She shouted, "Just push your way through. Don't just stand there. Come on."

I looked and still couldn't see an inch someone wasn't occupying. I then aggressively pushed the cart forward, and people got out of the way. I got to the van, and we met the waiting team at the hotel.

In Punjab

We were a portion of the larger team that had been assigned a speaking engagement for a women's conference. Therefore, our next destination required a train ride to Punjab. Lana began negotiating with the local train station porters to carry our luggage. The porters piled the fifty-pound pieces on top of one another, carrying two each on their heads.

Halfway to the train platform, they stopped suddenly and put the luggage down. At first, we thought they probably needed a rest from the weight, but then came the demand for more money. Lana began to negotiate. Time to catch our train was running out. Finally, there was agreement, the luggage was lifted up on their heads once again, and off we went in our best effort to keep up with their pace.

Arriving at our train platform, we realized there was no space for the luggage to be stored except inside at the very top of the train car. Thank God, Mel Boudreau was part of the team. She is a physically strong woman who loves hiking in the mountains between ministry and family times. Mel had to straddle two seats with one foot on each across the aisle and began to toss those heavy pieces of luggage in the overhead bins.

Our hosts met us at the train with open arms and the typical gracious Indian welcome. We enjoyed a time of getting to know the local leaders and resting for the evening. The next morning the women began to pile into the small room for the first women's conference ever held in that area. Capable interpreters translated our teaching, preaching, and illustrative sermons. The women sat perfectly still, intently listening to each set of speakers.

As Wendi began speaking, she informed the women that if they were experiencing evil spirits tormenting them in the night, Jesus would set them free. She barely got those words out of her mouth when a woman's screams penetrated the room. Our team members and the local ministers ran to her and began to pray. Wendi continued her teaching, helping the audience understand that they no longer needed to be tormented by these evil spirits. Freedom filled the woman's body in the name of Jesus. Right there in the middle of the sermon, the authority of Jesus was delivering and healing tormented souls of their nightly terrors.

Freedom in Christ

The heat in the crowded room was so unbearable, you could barely breathe, so I stepped outside to bless those coming through the door after Lana and the rest of the team prayed for them. As Lana touched one young woman, she leapt three feet in the air, levitating in a demonic manifestation. She was set free after we rebuked the evil spirits and declared the authority of Jesus. A woman who had passed through the prayer line exited the doorway toward me. She was staring and walking like a zombie in a movie. The prayers had stirred up the tormenting evil bondage. She began to manifest the presence and the voice of multiple demons. I sat her in a chair and commanded the evil entities to be bound.

Earlier, Mel had commented she had never seen an actual deliverance before, though she firmly believed in the authority of Jesus over evil forces. She was ready if needed to join in, standing in the gap for anyone else who needed freedom.

I asked Mel to look into the woman's eyes. "Mel, speak against the abuse, and on behalf of her true identity in Christ, begin to say lovingly and softly, 'I love you.'"

We had already taken the authority of Jesus' name against the evil presence and trusted the Holy Spirit to keep this woman seated and quieted. We had already declared God's love for her a few times. Now the wisdom of the Holy Spirit was to have Mel express unconditional acceptance, letting her know she was valued just as she was right there, right then, in this current state of mind. The more Mel looked into her eyes, speaking love to her, the obvious freedom from evil became visible.

In a sudden jolt of her body, the glass of water in her hands went flying. As the last spirits left her, she twisted backward, then slumped forward. Her whole body relaxed. The watching crowd gasped, as they realized it was God's mercy and grace setting her free. She was at peace. The Lordship of Jesus over evil prevailed again.

A Conference of Firsts

The conference was closing. Smiles, hugs, and loving words filled the room as we picked up our belongings to go back to the hotel that evening. Notable miracles had flowed as the local and traveling team served together that morning and afternoon.

The buttery naan bread coated in garlic at dinner that night was our favorite. We ate two helpings as we sat with the pastors and leaders, celebrating God's goodness. The lead pastor told us he had previously asked twelve different ministers to deliver those women, and they were never set free. But on this day in God's glory, Jesus mercifully set them completely free. We praised God together.

This was a conference of firsts. The first women's conference in Punjab. The first time the women there had ever heard messages aimed at their needs as women and on behalf of their families. The first time they had witnessed the demonized set free. The first time Mel had participated in a deliverance. The first time the onlookers realized how powerful God's love is when setting someone free.

You, Too

"The Lord is the Spirit, and where the Spirit of the Lord is, there is freedom" (2 Cor. 3:17).

"It is for freedom that Christ has set us free. Stand firm, then, and do not let yourselves be burdened again by a yoke of slavery" (Gal. 5:1).

"Let those who love the LORD hate evil, for he guards the lives of his faithful ones and delivers them from the hand of the wicked" (Ps. 97:10).

* * *

If someone came to you asking for freedom, are you confident Jesus' name and authority in your life would be an answer to their torment? Do you desire further training or understanding? If so, where can you find it?

....

Melonie Janet's Musings

Wisdom's chief joy preserves the life of another.
  In right time and manner, she rescues her sister and brother.
  An escape has been made from wickedness, madness, and folly.
  Conviction's lamenting and mourning in woe.
  In the heat of the Spirit, now go.
  Salvation's arisen in the land.
  Redemption has stretched forth her hand.
Open wide and sup with his pleasure.
  Walk in his Spirit far beyond measure.
  Wait until you're asked? No, now is the time to seek.
  Consider their need . . . now, consider Jesus, their hope made complete.
  After all, what is your chief joy and desire? Is it not to see their lives enveloped in holy fire?!

···

Lana's Leadership Lines

It's one thing to consider unity of the Spirit of God when working with personalities and supernatural impartations within team members. It's another to realize that the spirit world is filled with conflicting agendas of evil good versus evil, God versus evil spirits. When you witness this level of bondage and then watch the name of Jesus grant complete freedom, you can't help but marvel once again at the power of God's love. The unconditional price Jesus paid on the cross for us to be free from the devil's attempts to distort and destroy defeats any and all of his torment. The name of Jesus and forgiveness for ourselves and others, alongside unconditional acceptance, are keys that unlock living in the newness of life, resurrection life. Jesus is your Lord. You have authority in his name to deliver the demonized from bondage.

* * *

Thank you, dear Jesus, for setting me free. Empower me with your wisdom and authority to set others free from their bondage.

SOMEONE TURN ON THE LIGHT

Because He Said . . .

"And hope does not put us to shame, because God's love has been poured out into our hearts through the Holy Spirit, who has been given to us" (Rom. 5:5).

"So if the Son sets you free, you will be free indeed" (John 8:36).

"When Jesus spoke again to the people, he said, 'I am the light of the world. Whoever follows me will never walk in darkness, but will have the light of life'" (John 8:12).

*   *   *

Camarillo State Mental Hospital was fifteen minutes on a winding back road from my home. The hospital chaplain had invited me and my friends Kathy and Rob to be part of a team that offered a weekly chapel to the severely emotionally handicapped teenagers who lived on campus. Privacy issues kept us from being allowed to read their files, so we knew little about them.

Two Christian educators, John and Derek, had initiated the idea. Nellie, a Spirit-filled, jovial janitor, committed to join our small team. I often pondered their willingness to spend all day with these challenging teens and then extend it by ministering the love of God and the light of Jesus into their complicated circumstances.

John, Derek, Rob, Nellie, Kathy, and I began our weekly visits with an hour of prayer on campus before the boys arrived. Our chapel sessions were to be fifteen to twenty-five minutes in length.

These teachers and the janitor exhibited strength, faith, and patient compassion not only with the boys, but with us as novices to this type of ministry. Kathy was an anointed musician and singer whose music helped calm the atmosphere. As we spent time praying before the chapel began, I experienced a unique expression of the Holy Spirit by receiving words of knowledge or a significant gift of faith for their well-being. I began to sense what they were feeling and a supernatural overriding compassion. Praying with such a committed, caring team for these emotionally abused young men was a gift from the Holy Spirit every week. Over time, these knowledgeable teachers trusted us with the sharing time without attending themselves.

Ministry in a New Place

Outside of fidgeting and inappropriate comments, they didn't appear to be much different on the outside than any teenage boy. Each week, we designed a lighthearted message that conveyed a basic concept of God's love. Kathy would sing an original song she received from the Holy Spirit for the specific message we would give the boys. When it fit the story, a costumed presenter dressed up to add some fun, for example, a detective searching for something that made him happy.

We took turns being the storyteller. One team member, whom we secretly referred to as the bouncer, would wait in the hall. If one of the teenagers couldn't keep from excessively wiggling or talking, they would be welcomed into a private time with the bouncer. It was never disciplinary in nature. They were offered a time to enjoy a private session. The other team members sat among the teens during the story.

As you can imagine, certain trigger words could throw the boys into anger, pain, or rash behavior. The resident psychologists and doctors felt certain words we might use were too religiously confusing or damaging. We had to have an almost surgical precision in our word choices. The chaplain would inform us what we could or could not say. I think our limited approved word selection consisted of God, Jesus, love, and help, with a few more like comfort or happy. Scriptures weren't to be fully quoted but were to be taken to their simplest core truth and presented in the context of a short story. At times, we didn't agree with some of these restrictions, but we complied with their direction.

On the day I was to be the storyteller, the point of the lesson was the Bible is God's letter to us, and it has the power to defeat fear and hate. Dressed as a cowgirl, I buckled up the hand-tooled leather holster my grandfather had given me. Blue jeans, a wide-brimmed hat, and well-worn boots finished the outfit. I tucked a small New Testament in the holster.

During my story, I reached into my holster with a swift movement, pulling out the small black Bible. I pointed it at the boys, and before I could say my planned words—"You are loved"—the boys jumped up and flew in the air a few inches before they darted out the door, crashing through the chairs like rabbits running from a cougar.

I was shocked. It had all happened in a few seconds. *What had I done?*

The team chased after them. To my dismay, so did the staff in white coats with needles in hand. The boys were safely gathered back into their rooms. I wasn't given a chance to apologize or explain to the boys or their teachers what I had intended.

I realized later that a swift move of the hand from an area that depicted a gun in a holster was ill-advised at best. It was, in fact, a disaster, and I was at fault. Devastated, I drove home, petitioning God to grant peace and remove the pain I caused that day. How could I show my face again?

A Positive Message

Life has its learning curves. Finding yourself in one that no one can redeem but God himself can be identity crushing. It causes you to self-disqualify instead of picking up your sagging soul, trusting God for comfort and wisdom. As you keep on keeping on, showing up when you feel disqualified, a surprising, affirming message can, in time, appear to make the difference.

The next week, I decided to join the team again.

"We know you aren't allowed to read what they have been through and alert you to how they might respond," consoled one of the teachers later.

It was my turn to sit among the teens. The young boy to my left entertained himself by pinching my side. Wiggling is a light word for his body language while he sat next to me. His shoulders twitched back and forth while he kept reaching to scratch his upper back. Patience wasn't a problem for me. I was used to their out-of-control body language. Coming to the chapel sessions each week was a privilege they had earned, and I didn't want to cut short his time.

I didn't think through my next move. It was instinctive and instantaneous. I took my hand and lightly brushed his shoulder as if I were dusting off crumbs. At the same time, a few quietly spoken words in my spiritual language or tongues initiated a dramatic moment.

Startled, he looked at me with wide eyes. "You saw that, right?"

"Saw what?"

"That thing, that thing that was on my back. When you brushed my shoulder with your hand and said those words, it jumped off my back and ran out the door."

I made sure I kept my expression calm as if what he had just described wasn't a surprise. I gave the impression that it was a normal expression of God's love, helping him with his burden. I knew better than to describe the spiritual truth—that it was a harassing demonic presence that jumped off and ran out the door.

The story finished with the young man sitting quietly next to me, listening intently. Inside I was bubbling with grateful worship at what the Jesus had done for him. When we met for our after-session prayer time, the team celebrated Jesus' authority over the demonic realm and the freedom he had given the young man.

The next week, the chaplain said, "Janet, I hear you perceived a burden on a young man last week."

"Yes, I did. Actually, chaplain, it was a demonic presence, and the Holy Spirit set the boy free."

He looked intently into my eyes and said firmly, "Janet, hear me. You perceived a burden on a young man, and your caring calmed him down."

I understood what he was trying to convey. I realized that his description of the encounter was the only way we would be allowed to share what happened. Otherwise, mentioning the demonic realm would cause trouble with the resident professionals and confusion for the boys.

"Yes, chaplain," I agreed. "It was a burden, and God's caring helped him have peace and freedom from the irritation."

You, Too

"*But with you there is forgiveness, so that we can, with reverence, serve you*" (Ps. 130:4).

"*In him we have redemption through his blood, the forgiveness of sins, in accordance with the riches of God's grace*" (Eph. 1:7).

* * *

Where is compassion in Christ Jesus your Lord leading you to take authority over evil harassment in someone's life?

....

Melonie Janet's Musings

Sometimes love roars; sometimes love laments. Love always opens doors for God's full deliverance. Sometimes love is still. Sometimes love is fervent. Love always endures because God is omnipotent. Love's bravery surrenders, esteems others higher, even when their needs and inconsiderate ways seem to try her. Love is strong in confidence and quieted in peace. Love knows Almighty God is Lord of all and gives the helpless increase.

....

Lana's Leadership Lines

God does not despise the day of small beginnings (Zech. 4:10). The Lord rejoices to see the work begin. Offer what you have, and watch how he enlarges it.

* * *

Lord, help me be faithful with what you have given me. May it be used to multiply your heart in the earth.

FRESH EYES, FRESH INSIGHT

Because He Said . . .

"I was in the city of Joppa praying, and in a trance I saw a vision. I saw something like a large sheet being let down from heaven by its four corners, and it came down to where I was" (Acts 11:5).

"In a vision he has seen a man named Ananias come and place his hands on him to restore his sight. Immediately, something like scales fell from Saul's eyes, and he could see again." (Acts 9:12, 18).

* * *

In Acts 11, Peter describes his fresh and startling insight. First in a vision, God shows him a picture of an object coming down from heaven. As he watched closely, he saw animals and birds in a large sheet. He heard a voice telling him to get up, kill, and eat. His immediate response was absolutely no. It was against his religious practices and culture.

God caused the vision to appear repeatedly. Each time, the voice advised him about a change of mindset. He was given explicit directions regarding how he was to respond to the vision. God was preparing him with fresh insights into his love and purpose. The directions compelled him to reach into the hearts of those he once considered unreachable. God didn't let him get away with ignoring the vision. The voice from heaven kept urging him to reconsider his no.

The same gift Peter had received from the Holy Spirit was to be offered to a Gentile family. Gentiles were considered outsiders to the Jewish people at that time. Peter did as he was instructed. While he was telling them about the Son of God, Jesus Christ, the Holy Spirit enabled them to not only believe but also to speak in new spiritual languages, praising and glorifying God. Everyone was overwhelmed by the love of God as they began to recognize his heart for all humankind.

Has Jesus changed your mind about how he sees certain people or cultures? He has mine. Peter following not only the insight from the vision, but also the directives he was given was critical for God's will to be accomplished. Knowing his Word is important, but understanding his ways is pivotal as we reach out, sharing his heart for humankind. May the Spirit of truth give us fresh eyes to see and ears to hear what he is saying to the body of Christ.

Culture Shock

I live a couple hours from Disneyland in Anaheim, California. It's a blast escorting someone to Disneyland for the first time. When I was a youngster, I lived so close I could drop by anytime. In those days, it only cost a few dollars to go dancing as long as you didn't get on any rides. I had laughed, screamed, or become dizzy on those rides multiple times.

You know the saying, "Been there, done that"? There came a time when I no longer had any desire to go to Disneyland unless it was to escort someone on their first adventure in wonderland. Every time relatives came to visit, we took them; I went so many times, I had the place memorized. The surprise was that each time we took someone for their first visit, I experienced Disneyland afresh through their eyes. It was fun watching their enchanted amusement. Their delight became my delight. What I had missed when alone or from my myriad of visits, I discovered afresh when I viewed it with others.

Reverend Bing and Maryann, pastoral leaders over several congregations in the Philippines, contacted us about coming for their first time to the United States. I wanted them to feel special and began thinking of ways to treat them while they were staying with us.

It's not surprising that our different foods began to disagree with them, creating discomfort. What could we do to give them some fun? Our friend Rob was off work and offered to join me to give them a treat by taking them to Disneyland.

Entering the park is always spectacular for a first-time visitor. We wandered through the park's beauty and, after a short introduction to the massive amusements, decided to get on one of the thrill rides. Rob and I sat behind Bing and Maryann in the darkened roller coaster. As it swiftly plummeted downhill, an extremely large concrete-looking ball came flying toward us. We had assumed they would know it was only a visual effect and would never hurt them, but they shouted as loud as they could, "Jesus, Jesus, Jesus!"

By the time they realized it wasn't going to touch them, their senses were on high alert. They were mildly white around the mouth when we exited the ride. I whispered to Rob, "Well, that was a mistake. What can we do now?"

Then came the Matterhorn ride. This roller coaster is mostly outside with only sharp turns and some downward thrills. We had no clue how much courage it must have taken for them to get on another roller coaster. We sat behind the couple and watched the coaster jerking them from side to side around the outside of the manmade mountain. Now, it was clearly visible that the fight-or-flight response had set in. Relieved, we got off, and they bravely smiled.

We realized they needed a break from all the thrills. Maybe a slow walk through the beautiful gardens would be a good relaxing option rather than another ride. As we stood under the Swiss Family

Treehouse, they asked, "How did it grow so big in the middle of the amusement park?"

"Oh, it's not real. Touch the leaves. See, they are made of plastic."

They looked confused. We continued our stroll around the beautiful flower gardens.

"Aren't the flowers beautiful?"

"Yes, they are, but they aren't real, right?" asked Maryann.

"No, these are real flowers," Rob responded.

While we had tried to calm their frightened souls by a stroll through beauty, it added to their stressful confusion.

"Let's sit down, have a bite to eat, and relax a bit," I offered.

They had observed the park entrance prices but weren't sure of the monetary exchange rate. They had a sneaky feeling it was very expensive. Now, looking up at the lunch costs, it was obvious they were overwhelmed. They could have lived months on one entrance fee, let alone lunch for us all. The mental anguish seemed to be mounting.

Rob and I were praying, asking God for ideas that could turn this disaster into the blessing we had intended in the first place.

Rob whispered, "I got it. Let's take them on the It's a Small World ride."

If you aren't familiar with the ride, it has dim lighting. You ride in a small boat slowly floating in a waterway, passing various cultures depicted in painted scenery as you glide along. It's quiet, cool, and welcoming. The soothing music helps calm the soul.

"While we pass by each scene, why don't we pray for the countries they represent?" I suggested.

We thought this would tap into their heart for the nations. They were faith-filled, prayerful Christians with a daily prayer life for God's heart for the nations. So we thought it would help them manage all those adrenaline-pumping rides. They nestled into the welcoming environment, praying softly. After they heard "It's a

Small World" playing in the background a few times, they began to sing along.

> It's a world of laughter, a world of tears. It's a world of hopes and a world of fears. There's so much that we share that it's time we're aware, it's a small world after all.

God used this sweet international song to bring beauty and blessing into our time together. As we stepped back into the car later in the day, they leaned on each other's shoulder and feel asleep while Rob and I glanced at one another with a thankful grin.

Lessons Learned

It's a common reaction to have trouble stretching past our familiar environments. When we choose to remain in only what is familiar, it can leave us feeling flat and unsatisfied. It can also affect our eternal worldview. When a relationship has only mental, informational interactions, it seldom has a dynamic, compelling quality. When people extend themselves beyond their everyday norm, their involvement brings new sights, sounds, and smells, alongside a fresh, profound awareness. It enables them to lay down their familiar perceived barriers and reach beyond their past level of willingness to taste and see that the Lord is good.

My time with these precious friends taught me to see through the eyes of any upcoming novice team member regarding new stimuli they were about to encounter. Any brand-new experience has the potential to become a sensory overload if the training hasn't prepared them. While team members are out of their familiar comfort zones, it is my desire that they would gain new eyes and fresh insights about the beauty of God's heart and ways on behalf of people very different from themselves.

Every team outreach is enriching to a person's relationship with their heavenly Father. They experience him in wonderful ways. It often changes how they see their own identity in Christ, as well as the reality of heaven, alongside God's empowering love for people.

When I meet people who haven't experienced life in the Spirit, my heart goes out to them. I want to help fill that gap by introducing them to a facet of the Holy Spirit they haven't seen or tasted. I've watched it over and over again, what could have caused grumbling begins to fade away as they see with fresh eyes. They now have the opportunity to experience the power of God's love at work. Watching someone receive new sight from the Holy Spirit continues to delight my soul.

As I teach, preach, pray, and serve, God reveals his fatherhood, mercy, goodness, healing, and delivering power. What shocks most of us is that the Holy Spirit accomplishes these remarkable graces through us as we become vulnerable by saying yes to reaching out with him. It's an incredible joy to lead newbies into fresh, inspiring journeys, whether we go to the local park, canvass a large area, or take a trip around the world. I know they will come home different—expanded and delighted with fresh eyes and fresh insight.

You, Too

"Then he turned to his disciples and said privately, 'Blessed are the eyes that see what you see'" (Luke 10:23).

"I called up on the LORD *in distress: the* LORD *answered me, and set me in a large place" (Ps. 118:5, KJV).*

"Jabez cried out to the God of Israel, 'Oh, that you would bless me and enlarge my territory! Let your hand be with me, and keep me from harm so that I will be free from pain.' And God granted his request" (1 Chron. 4:10).

* * *

What new awareness of the nature of God does he want you to experience? What new insight is waiting?

....

Melonie Janet's Musings

What new mountain would he like you to climb to see the view on the other side?

What would it look like from his perspective and not just your own?

How could that change how you believe, act, or feel? There are endless possibilities, because we have an endless Father God who is ready to reveal himself in a myriad of creative ways.

EVER STILL
grown, I am still growing . . .
known, I am ever knowing . . .
filled, yet always filling . . .
to the fullness of the measure and
stature of Christ I am driven . . .

....

Lana's Leadership Lines

To enlarge means to increase, expand, add on. Reaching past current comfort zones enlarges your perspective. When God enlarges you, he is empowering you for entering new, unfamiliar land to see and do something you haven't seen or done before. Press through the fear until you find yourself at peace in faith.

* * *

Father God, you have not given me a spirit of fear, but I have power, love, and a sound mind (2 Tim. 1:7). Help me be victorious over the battle in my mind.

Connection, Conflict, Collaboration, and Celebration

Because He Said . . .

"He went into all the country around the Jordan, preaching a baptism of repentance for the forgiveness of sins" (Luke 3:3).

"Peter replied, 'Repent and be baptized, every one of you, in the name of Jesus Christ for the forgiveness of your sins. And you will receive the gift of the Holy Spirit'" (Acts 2:38).

We (Lana and I) each had brought four team members to work together at the invitation of a national underground leader in China. When we arrived, gatherings suddenly had to be canceled due to several dramatic and traumatic events. The nation had broken out in a sweeping, devastating SARS pandemic.

The Spirit Makes a Way

Our hotel's hallways and elevators reeked with the previous night's revelries. It certainly wasn't where we had hoped to stay. We considered looking for another hotel or changing our airline tickets, but the airports, trains, and buses were filled with people fleeing the country like drowning rats from a sinking ship.

We spent our time in prayer, listening for the Holy Spirit's directions. Our one Chinese-speaking team member, Ming, helped us navigate this conundrum. She met with a business leader who had remained in the city. When she returned, we discovered God had a plan. Our prayers were answered.

This powerful and well-connected business leader had given his life to Jesus and was agreeable to facilitating strategic God-ordained discovery meetings. His conversion was a complete turnaround from his past religion. When he found out Ming was a team member of a small cadre of women and one man who were Jesus followers, he was delighted to gather his colleagues to hear us share our hearts. Apparently, not everyone was planning on leaving the city. Business had come to a standstill, but to our surprise, the man's friends not only said yes to the idea, but they also were eager to hear about our God.

The city dwellers we encountered were more interested in keeping themselves away from each other or leaving the country than they were wondering who we were or what we were doing in their city. It opened doors of opportunity we had no idea could or would happen. Again, the Holy Spirit was working behind the scenes.

In our first appointment, well-dressed executives sat around a long conference table. Who were these people? What had they come for? We had absolutely no clue what we were being asked to do. It was like a 1,000-piece puzzle scattered around the table before us.

Introductions began, and Lana then turned to the person on her left and asked him why he had come. His answer was not only personal, but practical. "My wife left me, and I want her to come back. I've heard you know a God who answers prayer and know how to hear his voice."

"That's right, I do," Lana confidently answered. "I trust him completely to bring her home to you. When she returns, will you accept Christ as being the true God?"

"Yes, if she returns."

Lana dug deeper. "Why wait? Why don't you accept him as your personal Lord and Savior now and join me in believing she will come home?"

At first, he quietly paused with a puzzled look on his face. Then he simply replied, "Why not?"

The room was silent and reverent. He closed his eyes and lowered his head, following Lana in a prayer submitting his life to Jesus. He continued to follow her words, asking God to bring his wife home soon.

That's how it began. Simply and quietly, the Holy Spirit whispered into each team member's thinking the personal desires of and information about everyone around the table. We all heard from the Spirit. It seemed natural, organic, and reasonable. If they were shocked by our ability to read their past and present, they didn't show it.

We are still surprised and delighted about the miraculous way the Holy Spirit spoke into our and their lives. At the time, it seemed simple, practical, and easy teamwork. Today, we marvel at our boldness. We have learned when there is a gift of the Spirit filling our thoughts and actions, it's profound, but at the same time seems quite normal. The Holy Spirit's obvious caring for people became evident. Each of them not only became willing to know more about Jesus as the Son of God, but ready to open their hearts to his love and empowerment. It was one of those evenings, one of several days in that nation, that we came away stunned at God's ability to empower our complete lack of knowing. His providence was so compelling, our trust levels deepened overnight. Our teamwork was inspirational as the Holy Spirit wove us together as one heart and voice in him.

The team's petition changed from, "Now what, Lord?" to asking from a renewed confidence in his guidance, "What's next?" It was a glorious transition of soul and spirit working together.

The Love and Freedom of the Spirit

The word spread, and the doors behind closed doors began to open. We again spent another evening in a meeting room filled with a variety of guests invited by the prominent businessman. Located on the top floor of the building, the room had a movable divider, making it easy to put the women on one side and the men on the other.

Along with JoAnne and Lynn, we took turns sitting against the movable wall as intercessors. Testimonies and presentations introduced Jesus as the One who not only loved and forgave them, but who would fill them with the Holy Spirit. He graciously invited them into his divine purpose with evidence of miracles, signs, and wonders in words of knowledge and words of wisdom within his tangible presence. We grinned as the team of speakers brought their listeners into the beauty of life in the kingdom of God.

The last speaker introduced the Holy Spirit's cleansing and empowering ways. All over the room we could hear people praying. Some began sharing visions they were seeing in the moment with thankful tears or brilliant joy. It was their introduction to the Holy Spirit for the first time, and it was marvelous. Several people began spontaneously speaking in a supernatural language they hadn't learned, the biblical gift of speaking in tongues. Others were obviously enamored with his love, sitting with indescribable looks of peace on their faces. We could hardly contain the satisfaction we felt watching this holy and supernatural demonstration of God's mercy and grace.

One man stood off to the side in a corner with his arms folded, listening but obviously not engaged. Lana approached him and asked politely what he was thinking. No way was he going to participate. He described himself as a wealthy man, happy with family, and healthy. He said he had no need of our God.

About then, I thought I heard a small, soft voice say, "Help." I wasn't sure I had heard right. Then again, a little louder, "Help."

Lana heard it this time. We started to stand up when we heard a loud, "Help! Get in here!" It was Ted from our team ministering to the men on the other side of the movable wall. We both quickly turned the corner to find out what was so urgent.

All the men had gathered around one young man. He wasn't from their country or culture but was working in the city with them. He appeared frozen in his chair with his hands stiff in a crippling distortion as if he had severe arthritis. He was unable to open his mouth more than a quarter of an inch to answer our questions. We both had an instant "knowing" from the Holy Spirit what had caused this unusual manifestation: a tormenting evil spirit.

We asked Ted, "What did you do or say to bring this about?"

"Nothing," he responded, "except ask the Holy Spirit to come and make himself known. He just went into this stiff immovable state, and we can't seem to get him out of it."

When anyone surrenders their life to the practices of evil spirits whether in witchcraft or a myriad of ongoing sinful actions, they give evil entities permission to come against them in tormenting ways.

The Spirit of God is far superior and has authority over evil spirits. When the Spirit of God answered Ted's faith-filled request, these evil spirits took over this young man's body. These evil entities were trying to get the audience completely distracted or hoping they would assume the man had had a stroke or some kind of physical ailment. They were trying to remain in him so they could continue to tempt and take over his actions.

Only a couple of the men had a relationship with Jesus, but they hadn't seen anything so dramatic and confusing as this manifestation. They began trying to comfort him by treating the stiffness like you would a cramp. They gently massaged his arms and legs to release his limbs from this severe stiffness. Nothing was changing.

Making sure we didn't reveal what we knew from the Spirit of God, except to the young man alone, we began to whisper in his ear, asking if this particular sin had become impossible to resist and now was a major problem. As best he could tell us through the small opening of his mouth and a nod of the head, the answers to our questions revealed the permission he had given evil spirits to indwell his body and mind. We gently and lovingly shared Jesus' forgiveness and the power of the Holy Spirit in the name of Jesus.

The Spirit of God was demonstrating his love and freedom to all the men listening. In that culture, they didn't doubt evil spirits were real. They lived their lives trying to appease them. Now they would see not only how the enemy to this young man's soul had taken over, but how powerful Jesus is against the forces of evil. God's love was demonstrating his willingness to bring life and freedom. The young guy was convinced of the truth and began confessing his behaviors, asking Father God to forgive him. He committed his life to Jesus. He welcomed the indwelling of the Holy Spirit. When his genuine prayers were uttered, the demonic realm lost its power to invade and control him. His whole body and mind relaxed into a profound peace for all to see and be amazed.

We kept his secret. Nevertheless, the men saw and heard the power of the name of Jesus and the loving freedom the Holy Spirit can bring to anyone.

Ted is a wise, Spirit-filled man of God. We were very thankful when he took the new believer aside and shared with him the healthy principles for his new relationship with Jesus that would keep him free. All the while, the obstinate, I-don't-need-Jesus man was watching. Lana saw him paying close attention, so she approached him again.

"What do you think? Could you have done that? Do you have that kind of power?" she asked.

His whole countenance had changed. Instead of having a prideful, obstinate tone and body language, he seemed softer. In a newfound humility, he was still staring at the young man when he answered, "No."

"Would you like a personal relationship with the God you just saw heal and set this man free?"

"Yes, I would."

He, too, had become convinced not only of Jesus as God, but that everyone needed his love, friendship, and power to overcome the demonic struggles in humankind.

It was another glorious day of sacrifice, surrender, and surprises. All we could do when we got back on the elevator to return to our hotel was silently stare at each other, marveling at what God had done once again with his willing children teaming together to follow and find his ways.

Unexpected Baptism

We waited on the Holy Spirit's guidance each day in our journey leading us into what could be an opening to share the good news of Jesus, culminating in another wild and wonderful story to tell. Daily we looked forward to pivoting on command, remaining flexible and trusting even when we weren't sure of his voice or leading.

Looking for food, we discovered waitresses and a restaurant owner who wanted prayer. We saw God answer them miraculously. We were invited into apartments, and no matter how the evil spirits tried to distract or derail, the Holy Spirit opened a way, and we saw his caring for people revealed and lives radically saved.

As the trip was coming to a close, we were thankful someone found us a lovely room for a modest price. We would end the days with praise and worship, reviewing the details that only God could have brought to pass.

How we ended up with new believers desiring to be baptized we can't remember. All we remember is our hotel room had people changing clothes in the bedrooms, waiting their turn to be baptized. Our hotel room had a bathtub, so it became our baptismal. Our room became a holy sanctuary of God's presence. It was tangible and transforming.

God not only prevails as we lean in and trust him, but graciously manifests his presence in the most unexpected places. How do I describe what it's like to feel his all-encompassing holiness as the new believers lay down in the tub water, confessing Jesus as their Lord, committing their lives to his purpose and glory? What an honor to baptize these precious new brothers and sisters in the Lord.

Several weeks later after we returned home, Lana received an email from the man who wanted his wife to return home. He praised God because his wife had not only had come home, but she, too, had come into a personal relationship with Jesus as her Lord and Savior. Now, they were both growing in their relationship with God and attending a good Christian training center regularly.

You, Too

"Then you will know the truth, and the truth will set you free"
(John 8:32).

* * *

What are some of the truths about the spirit world you have experienced that have convinced you to become God's ambassador of freedom?

Melonie Janet's Musings
AMBASSADOR

The conception of Jesus within your soul shall rise up and make others whole. The very God of Abraham has stretched forth his righteousness through Jesus, the God-man. Deliverance in his hand, he quenches the devil's arrows and fiery brand. Empowered by his authority, you will still death's hour. Set apart from earthly and sensual gain, you are an ambassador in the kingdom of God; now reign! Equipped, filtered, and freed; a living epistle and creed. In furthering your Father's cause, you will wear the crown of heavenly applause.

....

Lana's Leadership Lines

Life with God is full of surprises. Some amaze us and are clearly ones that only God could have provided. Some have circumstances that can be hurtful, painful, or confusing. Scripture encourages us to be in season and ready when it seems out of season for the moment (2 Tim. 4:2).

As you face your clueless moments, your difficult dilemmas, and intriguing opportunities, look for his leading. Embrace his abilities beyond your own. Choose to trust his goodness no matter what you see or feel. You, too, will have stories that glorify him and reveal his ability. He will show you what he can do, in and through you, as you sacrifice, surrender, and welcome his surprises. Throughout my life working with international teams, 2 Timothy 4:2 has been a foremost Scripture keeping me always ready to follow the Spirit's lead when other plans go awry. Here are a few different translations of the verse:

"Preach the Word; be prepared in season and out of season; correct, rebuke and encourage—with great patience and careful instruction" *(2 Tim. 4:2, NIV).*

"Preach the word of God. Be prepared, whether the time is favorable or not. Patiently correct, rebuke, and encourage your people with good teaching" (2 Tim. 4:2, NLT).

"I can't impress this on you too strongly. God is looking over your shoulder. Christ himself is the Judge, with the final say on everyone, living and dead. He is about to break into the open with his rule, so proclaim the Message with intensity; keep on your watch. Challenge, warn, and urge your people. Don't ever quit. Just keep it simple" (2 Tim. 4:1-2, MSG).

* * *

*Jesus, the Bible says whoever the Son sets free is free indeed.
Wherever needed, set me free and help me know how to not only
walk in freedom but become the minister of reconciliation and
freedom you have invited me into.*

WAR-TORN TO RESILIENT HOPE

Because He Said . . .

"Ask me, and I will make the nations your inheritance, the ends of the earth your possession" (Ps. 2:8).

"Listen to me, you islands; hear this, you distant nations: Before I was born the LORD called me; from my mother's womb he has spoken my name" (Isa. 49:1).

"Hear the word of the LORD, you nations; proclaim it in distant coastlands" (Jer. 31:10).

*   *   *

Janet and I met Shirani in Perth, Australia, through Wendy Yap, a mutual friend who organized intercessors from around the world for the purpose of praying for the Commonwealth Heads of Government Meeting (CHOGM) in 2011. This meeting of fifty-four nations is held every other year to set goals for the good of the CHOGM nations. It is an impressive collection of leaders who are responsible to lead approximately one-third of the world's population. Even Queen Elizabeth II came to Perth for this prestigious and significant gathering.

Shirani stood out among the attendees. Her poise, along with her beautifully colored saris, caught my attention. There was something intriguing about her smile and sparkling eyes.

One afternoon after praying together on the river prayer cruise, she and I experienced a heart-to-heart connection. Shirani was lamenting that no one was willing to come to the war-ravaged area in northern Sri Lanka and brave the eight-hour road trip to Mullaitivu to share the love of God with those in need. As I petitioned the Holy Spirit for his leading, it became clear this was an idea from God.

Time to Act

Shirani supported churches, Montessori schools, day-care centers, and water purification plants in the war-torn region. She was continually subjected to dangerous and highly political factions. It didn't matter that she would at times have to face down bombings, intimidation, or detractors. She was a true shepherd in her nation. Despite the hardships, she continually served the believers in Jesus. Her efforts and coordination were to strengthen and unite them all in prayer for the expansion of the kingdom of God.

We began the planning in December 2011 to arrive in March 2012. Shirani had received special permission from the secretary of defense to take a group of ladies who were willing to travel north and go deep into a land well-worn by war. We traveled over 1,500 kilometers (932 miles). She was stunned that the team arrived still smiling. More than thirty years of terrorist war and the aftermath that comes with it had plagued the land, but now Sri Lanka was waking up to reconciliation and reconstruction. Shirani told us the believers in the land believe the end of the war came as a result of continual petitioning in prayer for God's intervention. Now, solutions to deep ethnic issues were emerging. It was time to act and to bring in a life-giving team.

I gave the ladies who attended our sessions small mango trees to be planted, dry rations, toys, clothing, and pillowcases embroidered with the encouraging words, "Greater is one touch from God than all the world can offer." The pillowcases had been prayed over by more than two hundred intercessors with One Touch Awakening and given to widows for their families.

We left Colombo in the early hours of the morning. By the time we reached Vishwamadu in northern Sri Lanka, it was obvious it had been a terrorist stronghold, as it now was in ruins. The two hundred downcast widows had patiently waited for us in the heat of the day. We were treated like angels of mercy sent from heaven. Traditional handmade brilliant yellow, red, and white flower leis were placed around our necks.

The smiles and dancing eyes of all the children made the atmosphere lighter and more joyful as they received a variety of small colorful toys that they had never had a chance to hold or even see before. Shirani reported that it was evident in the midst of the strong military presence, the love of Jesus flowed unconditionally. Hugs and cups of tea were shared amidst the giving, blessing, and comforting. You could see the military men who stood on duty were pleased at how we received the women and children.

A River of Life

The ride had been grueling. The welcoming ceremony was beautiful and uplifting. But when the tears rolled down the worn cheeks, from the faces looking so much older than their age, our hearts were deeply touched.

As we gathered in the tightly packed building filled with both adults and children at the Montessori school, I gave a message about the cross of Jesus about his unconditional love. Shirani was grinning from ear to ear, validating its uplifting comfort for the listeners.

She reported that she was sure it brought them healing. Why was she so confident? She said that many years later, women would still speak to her with such gratitude and affection for the ladies who came from a faraway country when no one wanted to come to encourage and heal their hearts. It meant so much.

Then came the celebratory mango tree planting to top off our time with them. Each of us had our own mango tree to plant. Digging into the soil with the help of one of the military men, we blessed this new fruit-filled beginning. Years later, she sent us pictures of the full-grown trees. As we write this story, Shirani again praised God profusely for the transformations she experienced with us on that mission outreach and wanted us to remember to thank the Sixty-Eighth Division of the Sri Lankan Army who made the ground arrangements and transported the goods.

Afterward, Shirani set up a conference for pastors and leaders to be held at the Vavuniya town hall. Again, the report came of a life-changing event for all those who attended. She said, "A river of life flowed once again. Hope was birthed, faith rekindled, communion broke barriers of unforgiveness, leaders repented, and partnerships were birthed."

The Urban Council Hall on day two had communion and deliverances from trauma and pain with inner and physical healing. The prophetic act displaying a silky blue canopy fabric flowing in the aisles represented the flow of the river of life coming to them once again as I spoke on the subject of God's glory. It's a remarkable sight when a visual aid speaks of God's wonder and personal care to an audience. His words are life, and the elegance of the flowing multi-shaded hues of blue waving softly in a breeze down the aisles were not only refreshing but also invigorating to the soul.

At 6 p.m. that day, our team member from Israel, Joan Lipis, taught on "Why Israel?" Many were anxious to pledge a new beginning in prayer for Israel, and two churches gave funds to plant trees in Israel.

Next we traveled to Nuwara Eliya, up into the mountains where the famous Sri Lankan tea farms flourished. We had a respite time and were treated to the honor of tasting the best of the tea world.

It was time to find our lodging once again. The lovely Grand View Hotel was a severe challenge for our bus. The entry road was so steep, it couldn't take the weight of the team. We all tumbled out with a big sigh of relief after listening to the tires spinning over and over in the ruts, trying to scale what appeared to us as almost a 90-degree angle up the muddy hill. It was too steep to walk without feeling as if you would fall forward any second. Somehow, someone found a vehicle that could carry a few of us at a time up that hill.

At the Smyrna Church (Pastor David Emmanuel) in Nuwara Eliya, Edna, Janet, Joan, and I taught several sessions with excellent interpreters. What a delight to have dinner at the Grand Hotel, praising God that evening in a room filled with laughter and deep abiding fellowship with our new Sri Lankan sisters and brothers.

"It's all about Father, Son, and Holy Spirit," said Shirani. "It's his mercy and grace. It is his love for his family, and we get the honor of being caught in the midst of it all."

You, Too

"The LORD reigns, let the earth be glad; let the distant shores rejoice" (Ps. 97:1).

* * *

If given the opportunity to serve in an area that is filled with violence and opposition, would you still go?

Melonie Janet's Musings
SERVANTHOOD

Servanthood in Christ is a dignity and a delight.
It is the torch he carries, the cloud by day, the fire by night.
While many in our day are saying that it's none of their affair, our Lord Jesus desires that we reach out and show that we care.
Don't inherit the winds of judgmental or apathetic attitudes blowing dust in the face of need.

Let the mighty rushing wind of God's cleansing truth
    be your passion and creed.
Leadership from a servant's heart
    has less to say than it does to impart.
In heaven's hall of fame is carved each servant's name.
Is it the price of entrance?
No, only a kind recognition of significance.
Jesus said, "What you have done unto the least of these, you've
    done unto me."
When we reach out to help others, our Lord takes it quite
    personally.
God's not as interested in what always shows
    as he is in what goes on when no one else knows.
Serving hearts have eyes to see and ears to hear
    what the Spirit of Christ desires and holds dear.
So, let our Lord Jesus' humble, loving ways
    captivate your heart and delight your days.

Lana's Leadership Lines

Leaders support their people and their teams. Leaders aim for unity in the Spirit in the bond of peace whenever and wherever possible. Trust God's heart for those you are leading.

* * *

Lord, it is hard to imagine the suffering of believers in war-torn parts of the world, but we have confidence in the mercy and goodness you show them.

Tour of Duty
2010: Afghanistan

Because He Said . . .

"Every place where you set your foot will be yours"
(Deut. 11:24).

"But you will receive power when the Holy Spirit comes on
you; and you will be my witnesses in Jerusalem, and in all
Judea and Samaria, and to the ends of the earth" (Acts 1:8).

*   *   *

Wars and their aftermath expose indigenous people to unexpected, life-altering change. Changes, in turn, create openings for the Holy Spirit to work in avenues once closed. Such is the case for the nation of Afghanistan.

Afghanistan is at the ends of the earth for most Americans. Twelve hours separate our time zones. Arriving in Afghanistan was truly a heaven adventure and a definite step back in time. I had never seen such a primitive country in both the landscape and culture. I realized that I was living out Acts 1:8.

Early in ministry, I began to sense the call to take teams bearing the likeness of Christ to nations that were far from what is considered safe for outsiders. In 2010, a local ministry and my church, New Life Church, invited me to take a team of women who were mature and bold. Kris was noted for being both. We partnered for ministry in a country known for danger: Afghanistan. Here is her story of our trip together.

* * *

The following is Kris' story:

Kris' Story

My son, a U.S. Army brigade commander, like sons from many other families in the United States, was headed to Afghanistan. No one, however, could anticipate that I, along with Women With A Mission team leader Lana Heightley, was also going there. Her team of stalwart intercessors were on assignment to help bring a Holy Spirit upshift to the nation.

The team's mission was to put prayer boots on the ground, to claim the nation for the Lord, working to see the good news infiltrate target areas through prayer, teaching, and warm hands extended to hurting and lost hearts. The leader of the organization we would be working with, whose name is omitted here for security purposes, told us how we should prepare for what was ahead: "Go in up on the balls of your feet, on the offensive."

On the Ground in Kabul

Crossroad nations like Afghanistan are created when cultures mix for many different reasons, including war. Afghanistan had been at war since the 1980s, first with the Soviets, then with warring factions within their nation, and then with the Taliban. When these cruel foes left, the country was in shambles. Bombed-out buildings, crater-filled roads, and concertina wire and military barricades lined its streets.

In 2010, Lana lead Sandy, Tina, Mary Beth, Debbie, and me into a nation of twenty-eight million souls still in turmoil. Our plane touched down in Kabul just hours after an explosion outside the gates of an International Security Assistance Force base had taken the lives of five U.S. service members. For the next several days, we would travel past that cratered spot almost daily as we moved in and out of the city.

On our first day, a young couple on mission in the nation introduced us to regional customs. Instructions included how to eat politely with our fingers from communal platters and how to keep our hijabs in place and our eyes lowered. The glorious connection with these young Christian workers was immediate and profound.

We also met a hardy band of expats living in Kabul, many of them teachers and medical workers, some having lived there for decades. The house church we visited kept its numbers small to avoid drawing too much attention. We learned that several other groups met around the city and had about 250 members. Within the next few years, fourteen of their members would give their lives in the land God had called them to love.

The team house where we stayed had an open rooftop that looked to the south over the city. To reach it, we had to climb to the fifth floor, pass the safe room, and step into the clear, high-altitude air of Afghanistan. Clothes had been hung to dry there, each intersection of clothespin and clothesline forming a reminder of our Lord's cross. The rooftop was a quiet, sunny place to pray and visit. Even in that private place, we had to keep our heads covered in case the neighbors might see and take offense.

From the rooftop, we also had a view over the top of the *choki-dar*'s hut, two metal cargo containers stacked on top of each other, one for storage and one for the guard's apartment. This guard station formed the front wall of our compound. It also hid from view a secluded lawn surrounded by roses and overhung by a grape arbor. In the early mornings, the streets outside were quiet and the air clear. As the city woke and came alive, the dust would rise, suspended in a cloud reaching as high as thirty feet in the air. This oasis served as a refuge from the dust.

The specter of a surveillance blimp monitoring traffic and guarding against Taliban attacks dominated our view to the east. To the south was a soccer field and the *madrassa*, a Muslim boarding school for boys who were often from families suffering from economic hardship and who were taken in to be fed and trained. The school was a focus for much of our prayer.

Kabul was a colorful community, thriving in its own way. One corner of each city block was used as a communal garbage dump. In the mornings, we could see children come to pick through the kitchen scraps. In the afternoon, the goats would forage there. Fresh naan, the local flatbread, was baked on the opposite corner. Afghans are nothing if not survivors.

God-Appointed Service

On National Teacher's Day, our team was invited to take part in a celebration for the Afghan teachers operating an after-school program. Some of the children were present for the festivities. As we chatted and enjoyed the celebration feast and music, a four-year-old girl stood and began swaying on her tiptoes. Just then our hostess walked by, snapping her fingers to the beat, and gently waved her arms to invite the little girl to dance. And dance she did.

As quick as lightning, one teacher scooped up a tamboura and began a rhythmic drumming on its strings. Another teacher pulled the curtains closed, preserving our privacy from prying eyes. Suddenly, everyone was on their feet. For ten glorious minutes, we danced joyfully, twirling like children, faces radiant with laughter. Then, as quickly as it started, in an almost orchestrated instant, the spontaneous celebration was over. Everyone returned to their subdued manners and quiet conversation.

What had just happened? Even though the Taliban's grip on the Afghan people had ended, the culture it had created through its totalitarian reign remained strong. Singing, music, and dancing had been illegal, and the enforcement was maintained by neighbors monitoring neighbors. No one was ever sure that someone else might report their activities to the local Islamic *mullah* and bring his wrath to their door. Yet that day, the God-given joy of life found a way to break through the bondage of the past. And the Holy Spirit had given us an opening to experience the Father's life-giving love with these pre-believers.

Another day, we visited the Kabul International School, where children of the most important people in the nation attended. We discovered that costumes for the yearly extravaganza were needed. The Holy Spirit had planned our arrival at just the right time. Mary Beth had been wondering what in the world she could do for the people of Afghanistan, using her gifts and talents. Within an hour, she had designed and created the patterns necessary for their costumes. The next afternoon, she sewed tutus, capes, and everything their school's drama team needed.

God provides in ways we can hardly fathom until we step out and into his wonderful plan. Colaboring with the Holy Spirit, trusting his plan, and being obedient to it takes us into places we could never imagine on our own.

Our ten days on the ground were full of other Spirit-ordained experiences. We visited an orphanage, did crafts, and played games with the children. Each team member had brought a planned activity to brighten the lives of these young ones. We also visited a community center outside the city that provided maternity care, a men's and women's clinic, a radio station teaching agricultural techniques, and an afterschool program teaching English and computer skills. Debbie taught a team-building class for some of the expats. We also met with a team of midwife trainees visiting from Youth With A Mission in Australia.

One day, the Holy Spirit anointed us for an especially moving opportunity to minister to those from other nations who live among the Afghan people. We spent the evening with a group of expat women, blessing them into deeper relationship with Christ through a simple Jewish tradition, a chuppah ceremony under a canopy.

Planting Seeds for the Future

One of our longest days took us three hours out of the city to a village where the *malik*, the headman or mayor, had sponsored a school for girls. In a nation where girls had not been allowed an education for decades, this school was a huge step forward. To get to the village, we passed through dry, barren hills and crossed a river gray from spring flooding. Finally, we arrived in a verdant, green valley. Rising from the dusty ground was a multistory adobe compound. Our Western, right angle–seeking eyes surveyed the compound's rounded turrets and ingeniously built structures, reminiscent of the Chaco Canyon in New Mexico, built a thousand years ago.

Inside the compound, we stepped into an ancient past with few evidences of modern life. The communal well and hand pump were overhung by ancient cottonwoods. A narrow lane led us to the heavy wooden gate of the malik's family compound. A donkey greeted us at the tunnel that led into a warren of apartments off a central courtyard. A lone, eighteen-inch square solar panel sat facing the sun next to a harvest of beans drying on the stone pavement. A 1960s-era television console sat in one of the rooms, nothing to power it and no antenna to TV signals. No one in the village of 1,200 souls owned an automobile.

We were received first by the malik's head wife in her apartment and were seated on cushioned *toshaks*, mattresses for sitting as well as sleeping, that edged the room. Our hostess lavished us with chai, a warm green tea, and sweet candies set at each place. This woman's prized possessions included a black-and-white photograph of her son displayed in a glass case. An ancient cassette tape player sat next to it, three tapes by its side. A hand-cranked sewing machine was proudly displayed, its cloth cover turned back so we could admire it.

After our visit, we were escorted to another larger room where we were introduced to the malik's mother, a very auspicious lady, along with several teachers and other important women in the community. Small gifts from us passed among the Afghan ladies and disappeared into hijabs and shawls, well concealed and kept for later enjoyment. Gift scarves we had brought were handed out, and then Lana taught from the book of Esther about every woman's important place in God's grand scheme.

The malik's fourteen-year-old daughter served us a meal. She began by rolling out a heavy oilcloth floor covering. Next she brought around an elaborate tin laver and water pitcher so we could wash our hands. We were then served platter after platter of fresh vegetables, rice, lamb, and naan. Dinner was finished with a delicious yogurt and dill drink. At the end of the meal, the daughter proudly took us to view her mother's handiwork, which was a large, handcrafted clay tandoor. A cylinder standing four feet high, it was used to bake their bread and cook their food. It was a masterpiece of engineering and skill.

Outside again, we walked along a river and enjoyed the shady trails through the compound. We were later escorted to an outdoor bathroom in full view of the compound's windows that overlooked the fields and other communal latrines. We thanked the Lord for the collaboration of well-positioned women and the modesty afforded by voluminous clothes.

While the Afghan people may not have recognized it, what we experienced that day was the beginning of a tangible upshift of the Holy Spirit's working in the hearts of the people, giving them longings for the new Afghanistan. It would create new opportunities for all people, men and women alike, and usher in God's redemption for them all. A year later, we learned that the girls' school had grown from sixty to eighty students meeting in the malik's house.

Behind-the-Scenes Mission

Living in Afghanistan presented rigorous challenges for the host and hostess of the team house in Kabul where we lodged, but they met them all with joy, courage, and grace. They kept the house cleaned and provisioned, and its kitchen operational, able to feed up to twenty-two guests at a time. They directed care for the guests, often from agencies traveling in and out of the country. They served as coordinators for the teams, meeting them at airports and arranging transportation and translators. And they were teachers and encouragers, often keeping long hours to pray with and support those traveling through.

While we were there, one long-term resident at the team house, a woman who had been on the mission field in several nations for decades, died. Our hostess, who was a nurse, kind minister, and friend to this woman, met the task of caring for her final earthly needs with courage. The host built her coffin, and her mortal remains were harbored at the team house until her burial in the missionary graveyard in Kabul. It was one more example of life in emerging nations, where things we may take for granted as being handled by professionals must be handled by everyday people.

After her coworker's passing, our hostess was unsettled, sleepless, and fretful. She asked our team to set aside an evening to pray with her, which we gladly did. She shared the burdens she could no longer carry on her own, so much and for so many years. This brave heart of a woman, a stalwart in the community, leaned in and allowed us to help lift her burdened soul and place it on our Lord's shoulders. Each team member brought a Spirit-filled prayer and a word of encouragement. This collaboration between us became a glory connection that brought deep refreshment, enabling our hostess to carry on in her calling.

Later that evening, we all went up to bed. I was sharing the room on the second floor with Lana and Debbie. As I stepped across the common area at the top of the stairs, I saw, in the Spirit, a figure coming up the steps. The strongest fear I've ever felt hit me like a bucket of ice water. Lana came immediately and commanded the figure to leave and never return. I saw it, again in the Spirit, go out the door and into the dark. The significance was not clear until our hostess told us sometime later that she never experienced another unsettled night and was able to sleep soundly from that point on.

To realize the spiritual oppression, harassment, and intimidation that rules in Afghanistan was monumental. But our team walked in the Spirit of the Most High God, and empowered by the Holy Spirit, we stood together and declared: "Truly I tell you, whatever you bind on earth will be bound in heaven, and whatever you loose on earth will be loosed in heaven. Again, truly I tell you that if two of you on earth agree about anything they ask for, it will be done for them by my Father in heaven. For where two or three gather in my name, there am I with them" (Matt. 18:18-20). Without the power released by that declaration, we would not have been able to do what the Holy Spirit had destined us to do in that nation that was so foreign to us.

Our team collaboration moved as heaven had ordered for this trip, quietly and behind the scenes, but in the power and authority of our mighty God. Our interactions were designed to bring blessing and refreshment to those we met, and we supported one another during the long days in unfamiliar environments. The team's alignment allowed us to stay, if not thoroughly vibrant, then aware and functioning. Above all else happening around us, every activity was encased in silent, ongoing, Spirit-directed prayer.

You, Too

"I am sending you to them to open their eyes and turn them from darkness to light, and from the power of Satan to God, so that they may receive forgiveness of sins and a place among those who are sanctified by faith in me" (Acts 26:17-18).

....

Melonie Janet's Musings

I threw myself in reckless abandon on God
And to my delighted surprise,
It was a sure-footed thrust.

....

Lana's Leadership Lines

Leaders are quick to adapt, adjust, and make hard decisions, even when outside of their comfort zones. They recognize God knows exactly where he is leading them. Their goal is serving God to bring glory, honor, and pleasure to him. They practice unabandoned obedience.

* * *

Father, I thank you that you never leave us or forsake us. You are the same, yesterday and forever. We can totally trust you with our circumstances. You are forever faithful. You know our future and are fully committed to our well-being.

Exploits for God . . . The Rest of the Story

(Original story found in *Upshsift* on page 101)

While writing my first book with Janet, *Upshift*, for the sake of integrity, I tried to contact not only team members to confirm the accuracy of the stories I related, but I also contacted our international partners to get their input as well.

In the chapter "Exploits for God," I was able to verify the story through our amazing team members, but I was unable to verify the details with anyone from our leaders in Zambia. If you recall, my star student at the University of Theology in Swaziland was a young man named Justin, the pastor who invited us to Zambia. I was in contact with him for some time after our meetings in Zambia, but I had not heard from him in approximately twelve years and even lost his contact information. Therefore, the book was published without his approval or input.

Our book released on October 13, 2020, and on October 18, I was astounded to receive an email from Justin. He simply wrote, "Greetings to you, Sister Lana. You have been on my mind and I found your email address. Special regards to everyone home."

I immediately replied to him. "Oh, Justin, I have written a book with our story in it. I could not find your email address to get your approval before it went to print. I will send you a copy if you want."

His reply was one of great joy and requested I send it. He was happy to relive the memories and laughed when he recalled how he tried to get me to reveal the questions that would be on the course exam.

A couple of days later, he sent an exciting email regarding the aftermath of the Zambian ministry. "I was reflecting on the conference you ministered here and some things that followed," he said. "There was tremendous revival and refreshing after. Many women got the impartation and were on fire for Jesus.

"There was one prophetic symbolism that has stuck with me. One of the women in your group took off her expensive ring and put it on the late Sr. Diana's finger and prophesied by the Spirit, saying that her portion was that she may not have a husband physically, but that through that ring she was married to Jesus; that God was jealous over her. A little later Sr. Diana went to be with the Lord. This prophetic act ministered to me that the meaning of it was that she was going home to be with her spiritual husband."

In *Upshift*, I shared about a very powerful woman who was a mama to many. She had supplied our team with materials to cover our heads when we faced the strongman at Victoria Falls. That woman was Sister Diana.

Justin wrote more about the promotions God had given those who worked with us and reports Moses is pastoring a church in Pretoria, South Africa, now.

ABOUT THE AUTHORS

Rev. Dr. Lana Heightley is an ordained minister with a master's and a doctorate diploma. She is the president and founder of Women With A Mission (WWAM), has been working in world missions for thirty-five years, sharing the gospel and discipling believers. Her passion is team ministry, raising up teams of "ordinary" women to use their spiritual gifts in teaching, discipling, training, equipping, and empowering men and women around the world to become spiritual leaders in their nations. Here and abroad, she is a mentor to countless pastors and emerging leaders.

Lana is the author of *UpShift, Presents from On High: Freeing Women to Walk in Their Gifts,* and *Divine Assignments: You Have One Too!*

Rev. Dr. Melonie *Janet* Mangum is an ordained minister with two doctorate degrees in theology. Since 1993, she has worked with outreach teams of all ages and ethnicities, both developing the team members as well as leading teams that train and equip in numerous nations. She has served as an associate pastor and interim senior pastor. She is the founder and president of Partners for Transformation, Director of Transformation serving in Aglow International, and is the author of *UpShift, Until I See: Light on the Path While Caring for Those with Special Needs*; *Selah: First Glimpse*, and *Selah: The View from Both Sides.*

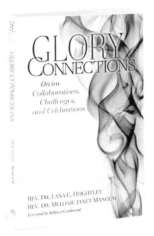